Tomáš Keltner
THE TRANSFORMATION
OF CONSCIOUSNESS

PUBLISHING KELTNER
2010

THE TRANSFORMATION OF CONSCIOUSNESS

The Mystery of the Cross

2010
Tomáš Keltner

ISBN 978-80-904708-2-8

Introduction

This book presents a concrete way how to free yourself from direct influences of those who are in control.

In this reality, there are many creatures (entities) present – but more than the unconscious mind is able to accept. Via the transformation of consciousness it is possible to provide the mind with such proof, that it would be able to get to balance with the soul and enable an individual to begin using their natural skills to their full potential.

The transformation of consciousness deals with the possibility of how to become free. Freedom as the basic presumption for survival. This book will uncover many mysteries to you. You may have heard about some of them already. Now you will also experience them.

I will explain to you how the principles of enslavement work in this reality – who controls human beings and why. You will see that we are not alone here. The truth – the light you have been looking for – is hidden inside you, not somewhere outside. You will see that you are not alone with your questions, your doubts and your fears.

"Oh, God! Why did you leave me?" It was and still is one of the unanswered questions of many people. Surely I am not the only one who can feel doubts and fear in that.

The answer is: "I did not leave you!"

If you are interested and if you allow me, I will show you how it is possible to get back this lost freedom. Through the information in this book you can realize how to be yourself.

The world we live in is changing. We are the beginning and we are the end, we are the Alfa and the Omega. The circle is closing and these who were the First ones are also the Last ones. One age is closing and the another is coming. We have the chance to create new things, create our own world the way we dream of – the New World. It is us – human beings – who can do it!

Fear is an obstacle to realizing. It rises its head in the times which are coming. It is not necessary to fight. It is necessary to understand what is really happening. Don't let yourself get confused. Instead of fearfully looking about, have a look straight in front of you. Be aware that we have skills people believed only gods have.

Let us get our faith back!

Faith in yourself, in the fact that we are not alone for all this. There are the signs around us which show the way. These are the angels you have been seeking – they are God's messengers.

Listen and understand:

You all are the Truth, you are the Way and you are Love!

You are the Light of the world and nothing will come other than through you…

This book is dedicated right to you.

Part One

objective

Freedom = Unconditionality

We start and end this book with this theme. In this book you will find a source of information for the transformation of consciousness. You will transform your consciousness and realize that you are free. You do not have to change yourself. It is the other way around. You will just be yourself, you will be aware and you will be capable. You will be free. You will soon receive information which will be useful to you more than anything else...

I am speaking about the transformation of consciousness and saying that you do not need to change yourself. Illogical? Not at all. Something really will change but it will be your own understanding. An inner change that you discover once it is happening. Rather, someone else will bring it to your attention. You yourself will feel the same. Maybe calmer and happier than before. Everybody understands a change to be an external change. Don't undergo this. Respectively, attempts to do so. In fact, it is not possible.

The basic presumption for what I offer is to be aware of who you are. This awareness is possible for example, through knowing who you are not. Certainly you are not the voice in your head. Yes, that voice which is now wondering what you are reading. It sounds nervous and tries to discourage you from reading. This voice which suddenly disappears once you start paying attention and comes back again when you are not being so alert. We will get back to this point soon.

This book deals first of all, with the intention of transformation of consciousness. It uncovers the way how to reach freedom – independency and the ability to create. We will touch on many issues but not in detail apart from the work with emotions and the creation of reality. Firstly, it is necessary to understand principles of this reality. If you practice the further described skills along with reading, you will experience unbelievable situations and signs which will change the way you think about this world.

The intention of this book is not to speculate but to show the way of transformation of consciousness. Everything I am speaking about here, I have experienced myself Before we start I will clarify the fundamental concepts about human beings which I use further in the book.

Man as a Trinitarian Being

You become a human being through embodiment of the human body. Embodiment can also be understood the way that the own being moves from an immaterial to a material sphere. This happens during conception. You choose your place on the planet, the family and most of all – the mother and the father. All this is your own choice.

A human being consists of three substances.

The first substance is the human body. It is like a container in material reality. The tangible determination of yourself in space. The human body has its own experience and also its own intelligence – its own genetics as a source of self-creation and information. DNA is a biochemical carrier of this information. In DNA there is what you have in common with your predecessors – from parents to reptiles. There is a lot of uncovered information hidden in DNA.

The second substance is the soul or the own being. The soul also has its own experience – genetics. But it is ruled differently than the body's genetics. We can call it KARMA. It is probably the most deeply rooted term of transfer of the soul's information between single embodiments. Most of all, in this field there are many facts and connections which are ready to be uncovered.

The third substance is the spirit. Your connection with the source. According to various systems, philosophies and religions it is what is called "god". Only the unity of body, soul and spirit brings full freedom. We will talk more about the spirit in the second part of this book.

These are three unchangeable substances creating a human being. Your actions are also influenced by other factors. The basic factors are a male and a female principle contained in each human being. Four elements – earth, air, water and fire – act in this reality.

Some other influences we will call present creatures (entities). It is a respectful term and it will enable us to communicate with them later. There are many of them. Some of them will be named earlier, others will be named later. We will give them names, for example ego or fear. Calling them present creatures (entities) I perceive as more convenient than demons, possibly shadows, larvae, negative energies and so forth.

Who am I calling these present creatures? All of those, together with you, which inhabit this reality. They are mainly information fields, energy-information entities which step into the decision making process in human beings and influence it.

First of all we will pay attention to those that are part of the human body and have direct influence on your life. They are ego and mind. All present creatures are very powerful because almost everyone is under their influence. → POWERS AND PRINCIPALITIES

This way we have prepared a basic overview of what a human is made of and influenced by. We will come back to these basic themes repeatedly, while we will be expanding our consciousness.

This is all my mind knows and understands

The Human Body

The human body is realized in the material world, so it is partly subject to its laws. Partly because other laws influence it. Laws which are not so tangible and are not directly recognizable in an ordinary way – by senses of the material world. The material world, in fact the world you think is the only world you live in and the only world that exists. Soon you will understand that it is not true.

The basic sphere where the tangible body is influenced by intangible frequencies are energy centers of the human body. They are most often called CHAKRAS.

We will briefly describe these energy centers of the human body. We will not change the already established name "chakras". There are seven chakras in the human body, seven main energy centers. In fact, there are six in the body and six out of body but we will pay attention only to those seven. They have defined relations which have been known to people across the world for thousands of years. Through knowledge of these energy centers it is possible to uncover the way to freedom. Therefore, this knowledge was purposely erased or very restricted in some (most of all religious) systems. The same goes with the teaching and knowledge of reincarnation.

All spiritual systems (religions) use the same principles on higher levels. No wonder, they work with the human body.

ROOT (RED) The first energy centre of the human body is between the legs in the area of the perineum. It leads downwards and upwards. It is the centre of connection with the Earth and the tangible world.

SACRAL (ORANGE) The second energy centre is near the genitals. It leads forwards and backwards. It is the centre of sex and potential.

SOLAR PLEXUS (YELLOW) The third energy centre is just above the navel. This is the centre of creation, free will, faith but also of mind.

HEART (GREEN) The fourth energy centre is in the chest – the fourth chakra is the centre of love.

THROAT (BLUE) The fifth energy centre is in the area of neck. This is the centre of communication and senses.

THIRD EYE INDIGO The sixth energy centre (sometimes called the third eye) is in the area of the forehead and it is the centre of extra sensory perception.

CROWN (PURPLE) The seventh energy centre is above the crown of the head and leads upwards and downwards. This is the centre of the spirit and the connection with the Spirit.

These energy centres are known as chakras, i.e. circles. It is because they are in fact energy vortices that move.

Their precise position in the human body is not very important for our work, nor is the detailed list of their aspects. You can find literature that will describe not only the position but also other details of chakras. These energy centers overlap each other and they are connected in a specific way.

Now that we have the necessary beginning and partial definition of concepts (behind us), we can move on to the substance of the transformation of consciousness. Firstly, it is important to understand how everything works, then to try it out and bring the proof to the mind. The mind will then not get in the way, and eventually, you begin to deal with yourself.

If you walk along this path then you will stand at the beginning and be enlightened. Don't think that only the highest clergy is enlightened and that it cannot happen to you. Certainly you sin and you are afraid and you don't even truly believe in yourself. Nonsense.

The enlightened, in other words illuminated innerly, is a person who brings to light (god's) all of his (dark) sides. He recognizes them and understands them. He sets himself straight, surrenders his significance, accepts and forgives. With respect to himself and to all those who take part. He now stands naked, hiding nothing, what or who he is or was. He stands with extended arms. Empty of fear and redundant potential.

This could be considered the definition of enlightenment. The truth is, that you can reach this stage. And right in this current embodiment. It is not only for the elected.

So, if you take this path of self-knowledge, there is enlightenment awaiting you. It is not about your position in society or a religious rank. We are talking about a state you will be experiencing. This is now your intention. To wake up from dreaming like in the movie "Matrix". Only in this moment will you really start to live. You may find this statement far-fetched. Try it but don't judge it. As one master of the martial arts once said: "If you don't like a particular technique, don't do it but first explore it properly."

GOAL { If you have gone through the first phase of transformation of consciousness, you are still in the beginning, but free of what it is not you. Not only do you know how the reality in which we live in works, but above all, you can choose what you give your energy to and what not to. You have discovered the first skill – you have started to influence reality, for now in the way that no one influences you.

By managing this skill, you will be different from most spiritual dignitaries of various religions and spiritual teachings. These dignitaries have wide and deep knowledge about this world. Some of them even know about things that have never been made public. But most of all, only in theory. The same applies for those who took the more modern play "being spiritual" as a means to prey on the trust of others. The difference between you and them will be that you will manage the skill and not "only" have the knowledge. This is the fundamental difference. The ego certainly likes this statement. It is true that this is the reason why I began with it. If ego likes something then it invests its energy.Thanks to this energy you will read further. But be aware, it is a credit, a fast loan. Ego will take its energy back with interest immediately when it understands the following. This may be the first imperceptible sign for you.

I will begin with what I have called you. With soul, with your own being. I am now talking directly to you. Only the own being is connected with divine energy. Only through the own being it is possible to draw from this energy. The energy everyone is interested in. Divine energy, chi, life power or whatever you want to call it. It is mostly about this. It is also true that it is about the soul. In fact, about using or abusing the soul. How does it happen? We will go to this immediately.

A human is born and is connected with the source of energy. Together with it – as its part (as a kind of accessory) – the ego and the mind start to be created. The two basic entities that are here with us.

The entity – a kind of creature – is in fact an energy-information field. It is an intangible entity. It is not something material (so material that we could see it through our eyes – a tangible organ of the body). However, it is possible to both work and communicate with this creature as if it was material. The fact that it is not material does not mean that it cannot show itself up to you, or that you cannot feel and sense it.

Several examples: Surely you are familiar with the power at a football stadium when excited fans yell some word together. When a football player scores. Apart from the fan's yelling you can also feel something else. Something which you cannot describe, maybe it can be compared to feeling of fear – if you are not taking part and only walking nearby. If you are more sensitive then you can feel goosebumps. Perhaps a deep voice touches you directly. You can sense this energy.

The demonstration of revolutionaries shouting slogans in a crowded square. The power of the people, the unity of voices – shouting whatever.

Remember the speeches of Adolf Hitler and the reactions of the crowds of his followers. Some authentic recordings are strictly prohibited, they are forbidden to be played. Such power had this man. But was it really only him? Today it is not a secret that there were groups of people in the military at the time which worked with hermetic teachings and magic. They studied both Eastern and Western teachings. They worked on strictly confidential projects. They did many tests and not all of them failed.

The army of Orcs in the film "The Lord of the Rings", their shout under the Saruman's tower. Can you feel this power? Just allow it to yourself and imagine it.

Do you want something realistic? Remember the hundreds of thousands of Russian soldiers during the Second World War who yelled as blood curdled in veins of their enemies. They often ran yelling without weapons, against the machine guns of the Germans' tanks. For sure you have seen them in documentaries. The stories of German veterans – many went insane – when this mass of bodies and energy rushed onto them.

During the Hussite war, the Hussite army had one powerful advantage. It was their singing. They were able to defeat five crusades sent in by the Catholic church against their reform movement. According to a legend, the troops of the last two crusades ran away in panic before the fight even began, as soon as they heard the Hussites singing.

You may be willing to admit that you probably sense something but not that you can see it. After the terrorist attack on the World Trade Center in New York in the US there was a photo spread across the Internet – a face looming in the clouds of smoke above the burning building. Trick photography? For mind, it's the only acceptable explanation. But this is what a present creature can look like if it shows itself, if its power rises above a certain limit.

It doesn't seem likely to you? There is in fact one other interpretation – an optical illusion or a coincidence. The magic formula hiding the truth – a coincidence. It probably was only a coincidence...

Coincidences do not exist!

Everyone needs different proof and everyone will get as much proof as he likes. Soon you will have your own. Only your own proof will convince you fully. Don't forget this when you want to share your experiences. Not everyone will understand or believe you if he himself did not go through it. There are many present creatures. In this book we will not describe all of them but we will talk about how to unveil their presence. This generally holds true.

We will talk about ego and mind as the first present entities. Their influence on the own being, the soul, is direct and can be verified the most quickly. Here we will start our joint journey for the truth and the transformation of consciousness.

How do ego and mind affect you? Through emotions. Dealing with emotions on a basic level is the necessary presumption for our further work.

Emotion

✳Firstly, we will describe what emotion is, how it arises, what happens with the physical body.

We will introduce an example that we will be using further on. You can imagine many different concrete situations, for example, a marital quarrel.

Imagine it is evening, you are lying in bed and falling asleep. It is quiet everywhere and you are breathing slowly and your eyes are closing. Suddenly a problem hits you. You recall a quarrel with your boss at work.

"He is such an idiot! Who does he think he is? I wanted to tell him that he is not right but he did not even let me answer. Lout. Everybody knows that I am right. It is not worth it for me to argue with him. I will leave soon anyway, so he can bother someone else. It is not worth it for me....
Anyway, it is unbelievable how he speaks to me. Only because he is inefficient and gives me contradictory tasks. I cannot do them all. If I by some miracle succeed, it still is not good enough – if I even understood what he wanted in the first place. Again and again he humiliates me. I cannot even stand to be with him in one room."

In a similar way – tens of situations like this take place in your head – memories of the past but also thoughts of the future.

But let us get back to your bed. There is a person lying down, his heart is thumping and he is breathing fast. His eyes are wide open. His fists are clenched and his whole body is in a weird tension. Maybe he is already sweating a little bit. Suddenly his duvet is too heavy. He is getting up and has to walk.

You have just experienced emotion.

A similar effect could happen if you are watching a movie. You are watching a new movie. You were told it is nice. So, you look forward to a pleasant experience. You are happy, full of expectation. You do not think about your boss at all. You press PLAY on your player and you begin to enter the plot. You want to forget problems of the ordinary day and for a while you want to move somewhere else and "have a rest". A beautiful story about the happiness of two people is beginning. You experience their fears and joys. You cry and you laugh. This all happens although the story has seemingly no influence on your life situation. The bread will not be cheaper and you have to get up in the morning and go to work anyway. By the way, it's the same if you think about the rollicking of the fans after the lost or won football game (notice that it is the same). It also does not have any influence on individual fans.

Just the same you perceive the happiness of the girl in the movie as if it was your own. If you watch a thriller or a horror – you are tense, your palms sweat and you breathe unnaturally. Why unnaturally? Unnaturally, considering that you are sitting in a cinema or lounging in front of the TV at home. But the "operational data" of your body do not correspond to this. They rather correspond to the reality (that presence) of the person whose story your consciousness (mind) is just experiencing and which may be fighting for dear life.

18

✳ Why is this happening?

We will go through this from the beginning. So, back to bed. You are lying in bed, falling asleep and suddenly something has attacked you. Here we will interrupt our story. Look at the last sentence once again. SOMETHING HAS ATTACKED you. It is absolutely correct. You were attacked, literally. This something is emotion. (Later we will specify this statement – emotion is in fact an exposure of the present creature's attack.)

In detail we will look at what is really happening. Something has attacked you. You were attacked. Most of all, it was your body which was attacked. What is emotion?

✳ **Emotion is the bodys' allergic reaction to mind.**

Your body reacts allergically. The physical reactions of your body are the proof. They do not correspond to your actual situation at all. That your heart is thumping and you are sweating like after a run and your muscles are tense like before a fight to the death. This does not correspond to the current state of reality around you. You are in bed and you should be silent, falling asleep. But the reality is different. Why? Because you were not present but mostly you were in the past. The problem was created; your own being – soul – was not here! If someone was watching you and telling you what he sees or even better, someone would film you, you could see your absolutely absent expression in this moment. You were not present! You were in a different time or (more correctly said) in a different place of existence. You as your own being, soul. Your body tied with this mate-

" PRESENT PAST "

19

rial world cannot make this trip. As a trinitarian being you are tied together and this division of soul from the body is very difficult for the body. Meanwhile, the differences of energy potentials – we will talk about them later – are being created. Your body knows that it is right now. It knows that it is in bed, preparing to rest. Then suddenly, without warning, someone injects poison (an energy poison) into the body. A poison in the form of a certain vibration. Sometimes you even feel that you are shaking with rage, anger or sorrow. In this case this vibration does not come from the outside but from the inside. You cannot hide from it behind a secure door. You are alone, by yourself, whenever and wherever. It is possible to observe this frequency not only if it is here but also when it is coming. Emotion is a reaction to a certain amount (dose) of energy that someone or something has sent over to you like poison into your veins. It floods the whole body through its energy system. The body reacts to this dose of energy allergicaly. And it starts to defeat. According to its own intelligence, and abilities. So, it reacts to information contained in this particular dose of energy. How the given energy waves are modulated. It means if the wave comes, then what flavor it has (how it tastes). This amount of energy carries an information value, for example in a form of conversation that happened in the past. The body attacked by poison (or a drug), perceives itself as present in the particular story, not in the actual presence of being in bed. The body reacts immediately according to its instincts. Are you arguing? Then a fight or an escape will come. The adrenal glands leak adrenalin and the body is preparing for a potential scenario. This happens on tangible level in the physical body. But this all happens as an allergic reaction on intangible level. The body suffers and is internally harmed. Its energy container (a certain form of immunity) is being harmed. Therefore you are tired after experiencing emotion. Not only externally – physically but most of all internally. This tiredness is connected with something else. It coheres with the fact we were divested of a part of our inner energy. And this is what is all about.

Once again we will briefly go through connections. Something has attacked you. This something has attacked you through emotion. That which went through your body and caused a reaction (allergic) was emotion – an energy poison. As the reaction you radiate energy from your body. It seems that emotion itself is only an instrument for something. Yes, it is.

Emotion is only an instrument.

The instrument through which something has attacked you. What is this something? It is one of the most fundamental questions. This something is a present creature. The present creature is energy-information entity. The entity that has the power to control an unconscious human. The result of this is that the first phase you need to reach during the transformation of consciousness is to emancipate yourself from unconsciousness. This book will provide you with the necessary information about how you can do it.

"You will recognize the truth and the truth will make you free."
John 8,32

So, we have the first contact with emotion. We already know what it is and how it appears – see the example of recalling the quarrel with the boss. I will get back to appearance of emotion later in more detail. That emotion in the story of the quarrel with the boss can be identified as negative. We can give it a minus sign. Whereas a plus sign is given to positive emotion. This is the example of watching a moving story or it can be some euphoric reaction.

Present creatures work with energy in its absolute value. This means that it does not matter if emotion has plus or minus sign. If it is euphoria or anger. Energy of emotion is the same both with plus and minus sign. In fact you know that it is sometimes difficult to differentiate laugh as an external expression from cry.

The way of how present creature's attack manifests through you is determined by what is energetically more convenient for the present creature at a particular moment. More convenient for the purpose of convincing your mind. Mind in fact gives this a plus or a minus sign. It depends on how it (mind) perceives a particular situation according to its experience. Plus and minus signs are not real, they are only a kind of description, a translation into mind's perception. Energy is the same, it does not change. Therefore, we can say that present creatures are not trying to annoy you on purpose (negative emotion) or the other way around (positive emotion). They "only" care about activating expenditure of energy in you, in the form of emotions. For this they need your agreement, consent you are giving to them.

You say that you have never given permission to such a thing. But how do you know, if you do not yet control communication with present creatures. You may even deny their own existence. Surely, they like this a lot. This is the way you can be controlled. Swayed by the mind and the ego.

Present creatures need their dose of energy and they will get it. Is it necessary to annoy you? They will do it without blinking an eye. Is it necessary to please you? They will do it with the same precision. The deal is made.

Back to emotion itself. We already know that emotion is an instrument of control. So, if you are controlled (through emotions) you cannot be free. You can flatter yourself, yes, but only until something happens. Until you experience another emotion, until you give up part of your energy to someone else. Until you experience some "misfortune" or you have some "bad luck". This cannot be influenced, can it? I do not agree and if you let me, I will show you more.

If you are not free you cannot control your own story. You are just a leaf on the water floating down the river. Some of you may find this convenient. For the rest of you I have good news. It does not need to be like that. You can become the one who creates his own reality. Not only a spectator or an actor of a story but above all, its creator.

It is clear that your liberation is the beginning of the transformation of consciousness. I call this state enlightenment. As an enlightened person you will be free from being controlled. For some spiritual systems the path ends here but the truth is that the path only starts here.

How can you free yourself? First of all it is necessary to begin with emotions. So, to stop giving your energy to others, if you stop giving away your energy, your potential will grow enormously.

From this moment we will get into the stage of practising. It is not possible to separate theory from practice. If you take this really seriously, then this is the point you have missed when you have read it before. Be aware that if you do not bring theoretical information into practice immediately, it will disappear. This can happen very easily while reading a book.

What kind of information do you already have? If you have not noticed it then it is the best to start reading again or to stop completely.

Yes, sure, a lot of information has been given. The most important information for you now is – what is emotion and how it happens. From this moment continually observe everything that happens around you. I understand you want to say that you normally do this. The thing I am writing about is that you have to observe everything that is happening and how it influences you. Only thanks to this, will you begin to touch softly – to perceive the truth. If you realize that you have just experienced emotion then congratulations. You have made the first step. To many directions.

How to recognise and realize it? This ability is fundamental. You can have a book which describes everything. The Bible for example. You can read it thousands of times. Maybe you have the theoretical knowledge of information that it contains. But if you do not understand this, you will only know labels, descriptions or containers of information. You don't know what they contain. If you do not transfer them to practice (do not live them) then you will stay a theorist. Although, a theorist with deep knowledge. The important thing is what skills you have. So called reading between the lines. But if someone does not give you interpretation, instruction, know-how, then it is very difficult to transfer knowledge to skill. Between those two terms stands realization and understanding. So, it is necessary to grasp knowledge, to realize and aplly it.

This book will take you step by step through this first part of transformation of consciousness. Doing so – we will uncover the first secret – presence. You can only realize something when you are present.

Presence – You Are Here and Now

Basically, I am saying the same thing three times. For a better understanding we will describe this through symbols. I will tell you something about the cross. The cross is made of two arms, two parts. One of its parts – the vertical one, represents space (here) and the other one – the horizontal one, represents time (now). The position on the cross in the middle, belongs to the presence. There – where time crosses space – is the present moment. Enlightenment and liberation is possible only in the presence.

In Christian symbology, which influences the majority of people, there is the Holy Trinity – the Father, the Son and the Holy Spirit. In other words, the past, the present and the future.

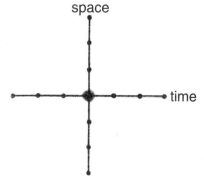

25

In Christian tradition, liberation (atonement) is possible only through the Son, through Jesus Christ.

Father = the past, Son = the presence, Holy Spirit = the future. You cannot but agree.

So, only through the presence can we reach the transformation of consciousness, towards freedom. This is the state that will not happen somewhere in the future. It is not important if it has possibly occurred and ended in the past. None of this will save you. Full consciousness (enlightenment or whatever you call it) is necessary to experience in the present moment, right now. In each "now" which you are able to catch and realize, it is necessary to be present. Otherwise it won't work. It is only about presence.

Why is presence good for us? Among other things, it can set you free. As you know, enslavement is related with control. Control happens through emotions.

Light and Dark

A skill (technique) that you will now learn is as ancient as reality itself from our current point of view. It is the skill (power) contained in the light. Divine power coming from the divine principle. It is the principle of not fighting. We will clarify this in the first example on the light itself.

If the light meets the dark then it does not fight, the light simply is. Result? The light stays, not the dark. Realize this. Examine this statement.

This being of light is a magic that you will be using. It will become a part of yourself. Because you are also a part of the light.

"And the Light shines in the dark and the dark did not embrace them."
John 1,5

So, how to use this skill (power) if you deal with emotions? **Emotion simply disappears if you use this divine principle.** What is the light in connection with emotion? **Light is the presence and emotion is the dark.** In the presence of light, dark does not exist. In your conscious presence emotion does not exist. Dark simply disappears if light comes. Emotion will simply disappear if you do not identify yourself with it in any way. To identify means to let it influence or to fight it. To disagree, to have "your own" opinion, or view of a thing. Does the light deal with the dark anyhow? Does it fight with the dark possibly? Not at all, light simply is. Dark does not die or anything like that, dark is simply not in the presence of light. This is the pure truth. I did not discover it. It is written in many books, both old and modern. But this is the problem. It is such well known information that nobody deals with it anymore. In paradox, it may not be so familiar anymore. This would not matter if everyone would have lived this information, would have realized it in their own reality. But this has not happened. So, if I would want to pass over this most fundamental information, I have just done it. Result? Nothing. The reader will take out of this only the fact that this information exists. The reader will react through his mind – he will either accept the information or deny it. Nothing will have changed. The reason I am writing this you will understand later. Maybe after you read this book again in a different phase of consciousness than in which you are now.

Simply said – I am repeating myself on purpose – if you give only information, even if it is perfectly correct and true, it does not need to be understood and realized well. The reader may not realize the information which is a necessary presumption to accept it and live it. Presence is the key to many skills.

Presence
(WHERE INFINITE POSSIBILITIES EXIST)

What is presence actually? Firstly, let's say what it is not. **A flashback is not the presence.** Notice that in our first story about the boss, it was also a flashback. It was a memory of a particular situation, a discussion with your boss at work. At the moment when you had started dealing with the flashback, your state began to change. The more you were present in the past the more you were reacting – your body reacted to "the reality" in which you had found yourself. The present creature which produced this play (in this case, ego) had used this divine principle (presence) and its energy (with your consent, of course) to make a past experience real. The past experience which already happened and is not in your current presence anymore!

In other words, the present creature influenced reality and created another one. Such reality that brings it satisfaction. Concretely, the reality in which you experience emotions that feed this present creature. The reality was manipulated! Through you, using divine energy. Exactly in this way reality is being influenced, you become "god" in a way. We will pay attention to this topic in the second part of the book.

Through this example you can see how it happens. So, a flashback is not the presence. The flashback calls into action situations and processes that are in a different place in existence than you. Your body reacts to this fact. The body that is directly connected with the material part of this reality cannot travel through time (more precisely – through space). The problem is speed, where the speed of light is the limit for mass. This is not fact, it is only an outspoken presumption. Outspoken – in fact realized (influencing further).

Considering that you, as a trinitarian being, dispose of other substances than the body that are fully independent (though directly connected). In one moment you can transfer yourself in space (for your understanding, imagine in time) to another place. You transfer yourself, your own being, who you are. Your soul if you want. You do this freely, in fact – very often because of someone's impulse. But because this is not an attempt from inside (controlled by yourself) but from outside (controlled by a present creature), your body perceives it as an attack and reacts according to its instincts. Instincts typical for the reality in which the body is. The instincts of the body are connected with everything that has been experienced (anytime and anywhere) and what has been reacted to. The intelligence of the body chooses how to react from this repertoire.

You are lying in your bed and something has attacked you. Very quickly, images and sound, the whole environment and backdrop are realized – you perceive this with your whole body that YOU ARE there. In the office in front of your boss. It is like snapping your fingers and suddenly you are there. Such power you have! This all happens from your side "unconsciously". Consider what possibilities will open for you if you control this consciously...

You Are Lying in Bed and
Something Has Attacked You

Now you know that you were attacked by a present creature. Its motivation is to gain something for itself, its existence, "thanks to" you – energy. It is not motivated by anger, revenge or anything like that. Simply, the creature is "hungry" (needs) and you have the food (you have what it needs). The creature asks if it can take it. You say yes. Then the scenario which we described in the beginning, is played out.

The shepherd goes and shears a sheep. He gets its wool which he can further use for his profit. Not for the sheep's profit. The sheep is cold for a while but it gets over it (it is supposed to be like that) and its wool grows back. The shepherd comes again and this is repeated over and over until the sheep (shepherd) dies or leaves.

This is an example of when ego draws from your energy, like the example of the discussion with your boss. You don't only agree to it but you in fact need it. Isn't that nonsense? You don't have the need to argue? But the sheep needs to be sheared. Ask the shepherd what happens if he doesn't do it...

In this context we can also describe another example. Emotion experienced while watching a movie. Again, some present creature draws your energy through your emotion.

It is like milking a cow. A wise farmer comes, touches the cow and asks. The cow agrees. The farmer sits down and milks the cow. He even makes the cow feel good. He takes redundant energy (milk) away from the cow which could cause trouble for the cow if it isn't milked.

How is this connected? Directly. In this context, human beings are the milk cows and the present creatures are the farmers. This story of the cow is easier to understand. Milk which is not milked can cause so much trouble that the cow can die. Why is this like that? It doesn't have to be like that. Nobody shears sheep and milks cows that live freely in the countryside. This need was created by a man (human – creator – god) when he began to control them. We could logically assume that a human can also have problems if he is not drawn of his energy (if he is not "milked").

Yes, this alternative is still in play. But human beings are not yet in the phase where this would be irreversible. They are very close and that is why it is necessary to start doing something about it. What? To realize, what is happening.

Gods Shepherds

One very fundamental event happened at the time when (at the place where) humans lost their freedom ("the expulsion from Paradise"), they did not however lose their divine origin. Human beings have not always been the way they are today. They were perfect like small children of today. We can compare this perfection to a plain canvas. An artistic genius is capable of creating a masterpiece on such a cloth, or perhaps not. A human being who has come to knowing was at one time also like a plain sheet of paper, a plain canvas. Through knowledge, by the intervention of Lucifer, mind was created. Mind had started to exist and because everything was pure, the mind had a free reign. At that time there were many gods, entities on Earth. Entities existing on other frequencies. It has been millions of years – millions of years the way we perceive them today. Some mystics say it was 300,000 years ago. It is not important when it was exactly. Time runs differently at different places of existence. Therefore this information is as relative as the calendar that the Jews use when they count years from "the creation of the world". This creation is the moment I am writing about. It was about forming of only this reality, not of the whole existence itself.

Right from these times comes all of today's known knowledge, transferred in different forms in different parts of this planet. These gods, we will be calling them Shepherds, experimented in this reality with humankind and also with themselves. A huge amount of energy had been released during those experiments and at the same time a big amount of energy was needed for all of this. Shepherds had been using human beings, their connection to the core, to God. They used people for the production of this divine energy and they used this energy in the way that they wanted. It was necessary to mutate the genetics of people at the level of a physical entity, so that they could control them. Out of the twelve energy-information gates that human beings would have been able to use fully, only two gates have remained partly functional. It is the same with DNA helixes. Those gods needed human beings but not in a conscious form. They needed them as a tool for their intentions. It was then necessary to decrease the level of spiritual awareness in a human being. Above all, through newly created mind it was possible to control (through its place of realization – through the brain – see further).

Gods Shepherds had transformed themselves, left or stayed in different forms People with their natural ability to be in contact with divine energy remained. Even the energy itself remained. Its unprocessed parts. Because the energy was originally from God (Existence), it had also had a schema of a human being in its "genetic" information. With everything that belongs to it, of course. This "free" energy had gradually started to realize itself. It had started to exist as a certain entity. It had started to perceive itself as an entity and realized also the ability of decision making. Evolution went further. Similar entities had started to form and group their "sheep" – people, around themselves. Religions had started to rise, the way we know them today. Here we will finish with this very brief description.

The question is what to do with it. And this is what is now necessary to deal with.

Now you know what the analogy is between a man "milked" by a present creature and a sheep that is sheared by a shepherd or a cow that is milked by a farmer. The comparison to the discussion with your boss may not be immediately understandable. But the second example, of watching a movie is. In fact, you go fully consciously to watch a movie, knowing beforehand that you will experience emotion. And that is why you go there – to experience it. You have no idea how much you poison your physical body by doing so.

I have said that a cow needs to be milked. In fact, it is the same with a human. So, if he is not able to control his energy by himself, then it is comprehensible that he allows "milking". The same way a cow (in principle) gives permission to the farmer to be milked. The same way a sheep gives permission to the shepherd to be sheared. You might say that nor do sheep neither cows need this naturally. And you are absolutely right. The transformation of consciousness is just uncovering this truth to you. It is bringing you the awareness that you don't need this either.

The Word Presence

Another divine technique or power, by which consciousness is endowed, is the word. **The word creates.**

"In the beginning was the Word."
John 1,1

What is meant is the beginning of this reality. To the first and simple question – who uttered this word – religion has an immediate and the same simple answer – God. It continues:

And God said, "Let there be light," and there was light.
Genesis 1,3 (1st book of Moses)

Here we will not deal with the hidden manipulation of the Church included in the Bible but we will focus on the truth that the Bible contains.

In fact, we will not do it without a certain completion. It is only difficult to find the truth and to interpret it correctly without certain powers. How is it possible that someone manipulates a text and not the truth itself? If someone manipulates, then he is not at the top level of consciousness. From a certain point of view he is not a master but at most, a very advanced student. Therefore he can influence and manipulate only up to the level of his consciousness (although that can be very high), but not higher. Such a manipulator, as anyone else, cannot give what he does not have himself.

As I have said you need to be capable to recognize the truth and not to get confused by a concrete interpretation. The certainty is God, Existence itself. As he is Existence, he is also the truth, light and love. The truth in its endless power simply has endless energy and this is "more" than any power of any manipulator, even if he was by present creatures.

It is simple. As we have described above – **light is** and if someone creates shadow with the help of mass, this shadow is not different light. Light does not drop shadows. **Shadow is not dark light**, shadow is only shadow, so it is the absence of light, not different light. Light remains light and it is enough if you walk a little bit – and change the angle of the beam of light. The shadow will again disappear. Without a fight. It is the same with the truth because the truth is the light. Shadow is like a picture in a mirror. It can seem as perfect as what it is reflecting. It can rouse the perception that it is alive. But still, it is only a picture, it is not alive. The same with shadow – it is not the light or a different kind of light.

Therefore the light does not fight with shadow, it isn't possible, shadow isn't alive. In the presence of the light shadow simply does not exist. There is nothing to fight with. Be aware of this!

The end result is that truth cannot be changed or destroyed just as the light cannot. It can be wrapped in allegories, manipulated and through different techniques concealed under a cloak of darkness (unconsciousness). But there is no such night after which morning does not come.

Gradually we will dig deeper and deeper into the truth. Such wide consciousness you need to get closer to the truth. A brief statement of facts, although true, would not take you anywhere. Already by reading this book you are going through the transformation of consciousness. The transformation is happening via these words at all levels of your own being's existence.

So far we have only touched on some topics that have direct connection with the first phase of awareness. During the transformation of consciousness everything will show itself to you. All of a sudden you will find out that you have realized something. As without any effort, as if by chance. And that is what it is about.

The word creates. Whatever you say is a slung arrow that flies and creates. Nothing is not only just something. Everything you say carries the same significance. It is important you to be aware of this fact. By what you say, you create your own reality, your own life. I will describe this with a simple example that is widely used these days. Surely you will soon understand why.

We will examine the statements: "It is dreadfully beautiful." and "It is terribly pretty." Do you take them as perfectly normal expressions for something you really like? Then you are very much off base. This mistake costs you more than you realize.

Let me explain why. You say "dreadfully beautiful" and you mean something pleasant. Not at all. In fact you are summoning DREAD (fear), one of the most powerful present creatures. In the word "dreadfully", dread is hidden. Why is it that you connect "beauty", in fact admiration, with fear!? Because everyone does it? Of course, because they don't know what they are doing!

You pronounced a curse in which you invoke fear. You are calling it into your life. It comes as it is invited. You did not mean it like that? Ignorance of law is no excuse. Those are the defined rules, your rules, you remember...

So by saying "dreadfully beautiful" you are inviting dread, fear into your reality. By the second statement "terribly pretty" you are conjuring horror to be present at everything that is pretty. Do you understand? The word creates. Whatever you say, creates.

Let's look at an example from the business world. There can be two people sitting next to each other who at first glance seem much the same. One is "doing well" and the other one is "not doing well". What is the diference between them? In what each of them believes in. If everything is a problem and everything is already being done by someone else, competition is fierce and he only has a small chance which depends on whether he will be "in the right time at the right place" or not. The second possibility is not to allow such images and you will be living your "American dream" – your heaven on Earth – right now. You will simply do well and you will always be "in the right time at the right place". Others will be saying that it isn't possible. Why is it that you broke through in this field? How is it possible that someone completely unknown wins an Oscar, how come that an unknown athlete defeats professionals who know "everything"? Such as when there was a huge boom of African athletes years ago. Where is the difference, "this coincidence"? Who or what causes that someone, although he knows all market analysis, and goes to a winning battle, all of the sudden loses and some "dreamer", who did not do as much for it, wins? This is what I am shedding light on in this book. I am giving not only a description but also practical guidance.

These are the ancient rules of existence. Magicians are aware of this. You create by word. You sin by word. Do not do it, try not to do it and you will be surprised how your life will change.

Again, I am not saying anything new. The ancient Toltecs knew the power of the word. You know it too, of course. Only you do not fully realize it.

"Listen to me, everyone, and understand this! Nothing outside a man can make him unclean by going into him. Rather, it is what comes out of a man that makes him unclean."
Mar 7,14

Why people have been using words created on the basis of fear and dread to determine quantity, eventually peace, quality and degree? Why do they say: "dreadfully beautiful" or "terribly pretty"? It is manipulation through fear which has been carried out by gods for ages. Directly and indirectly. The Bible is full of punishing gods. Man is pictured there as a powerless blade of grass hurled by the wind. Turned adrift. It is contained in the multivocal statement: "For dust you are and to dust you will return."

Jesus of Nazareth and others would be surprised if they would read the Bible the way it has been translated today.

No, Jesus would not be surprised. Jesus as the entirely conscious being had access to Existence (God) and the knowledge which it contained. So, he knew.

As he knew about Judas Iscariot, he knew the story in which he would be abused. Let me use the quotation from the Gospel of Judas not registered by church, where it says among others (amended):

Apostles speak about their vision:

"We have seen a great house with a large altar in it, and twelve
men—they are priests. And a crowd of people is waiting
by that altar, until the priests come and receive the
offerings.

Some sacrifice their own children, others their wives,
in praise with each other;
Some sleep with men;
some are involved in slaughter;
some commit a multitude of sins and deeds of lawlessness.
And the men who stand by the altar, invoke your name
(Jesus).

Jesus answers:

"Truly I say to you, all the priests
who stand by that altar invoke my name.

That is the god you serve,
and you are those twelve men you have seen.
The cattle you have seen brought for sacrifice are
the many people
you lead astray,
And generations of the pious will remain loyal to him.
After him another man will stand there from
the fornicators,
and another will stand there from the slayers of children,
and another from those who sleep with men,
and those who abstain,
and the rest of the people of pollution and lawlessness
and error,
and those who say, 'We are like angels';
They are the stars that bring everything to its conclusion.
For to the human generations it has been said,
'Look, god has received your sacrifice from the hands
of a priest.'

That is, a minister of error.

On the last day they will be put to shame."
Judas 38–40

The above mentioned text implies that Jesus was aware of the exploitation of his name. It seems that even this text was manipulated in a certain way but not the truth that it contained.

It is mentioned that, "it has been said". In the beginning was the Word. God said: "Let there be light." Can you see it there? It is about what you say. The key is to understand the words, in fact, their real (sometimes at first sight hidden) meaning. In the following chapters I will be drawing to your attention words of which you will need to realize their true meaning of.

By the interpretation, understanding and realization of their meaning you will be gaining another new divine power. These are the principles that also uses magic in its teaching. This is not bad for us. It is only necessary to become aware of it. What is magic in fact? If we ignore tricks, in fact cheating, based on ignorance or the inability of the viewer to observe something, magic is a crosspoint between the physical and the metaphysical, between intangible and tangible. It is a process where you materialize the intangible. Magic is very powerful. Therefore, deal with magicians at eye level, always with respect but without fear.

I will cite one more quotation which is from the Smaragdine Table:

Tabula Smaragdina, the author Hermes Trismegistos (god Thoth):

"That which is below is like that which is above that which is above is like that which is below to do the miracles of one only thing."

You can use this broad-spectrum quotation for your realization of the power of the Word. Not only God can create by word but you also can. In fact you have already been creating your reality, your life situation in which you are now.

So, start listening to what you say and realize that (and above all what) you create with it. In the beginning it is enough if you notice words such as "terribly" and "dreadfully" in your surroundings and of course you should try to avoid them in your speech.

Past, Present and Future

Let us continue on the path of the transformation of consciousness by being aware of the basic principles and ways of controlling of your own being.

We have said that for the control of divine energy flow which you have, projections outside the present are used. Projections of either the past or the future. Because you start to cooperate, you fall into a trap set by the one who wants to manipulate you. In fact, you are giving permission to be plundered of part of your energy. There is an analogy with energy vampires which modern psychology deals with. Yes, it is like that. But we are dealing with the process itself, with its trigger and with everything involved. Only this way you can understand and fully realize the power which is hidden in it. If we were not dealing with this theme in detail, you would not be able to realize other issues.

In the moment when someone (something) needs your energy for itself or (beware!) needs to weaken you, then it uses projections of the past or the future. We can voice the fact that: **projections of the past or future are used for controlling of the own being**. What does it mean? If someone or something wants to control you, then it shows a holographic projection of processes to you, which happened in past (in another place of existence) or which could happen in future. Examine this. It is a great knowledge that you will be using further.

Let's go back to our story with the boss. The present creature, in this case ego, projected (showed a movie) to your imagination – the discussion you had with your boss sometime in the past (this morning). Your body reacted in an allergic way to the mind that started to co-operate with ego. Mind accepted that the watched projection is real. At that moment you (your own being, soul) moved to the past and experienced a process there. Your physical body is not able to do so. Distortion, disassociation, tension of present reality relations occur. From the observer's point of view you are lying in your bed, you have an absent expression and your body is behaving "weirdly". Weirdly from the observer's view, who can "only" see through their eyes, tangible reality, part of the presence. If they used extra sensory perception, they could "see" more. This means that your own being is separated from your body, dissociation of the body and the soul. The body reacts to information from the mind that is watching the movie showed to you by ego. The movie is the story about the dialogue with your boss. Divine energy which you have at your disposal is released during this process. In fact, this all happens only for this reason. Energy is released to enable travelling of your own being (soul) and to keep the soul in touch with the body. This way emotion arises. Emotion which is a poison for your body.

This poison, emotion comes through the whole body and poisons it. The body tosses. At intangible level, energy radiates from the body and is perceived by the present creature that caused all of this. If I do not dismiss that you have caused it by your (unconscious) agreement to this process. In this way the present creature draws your energy away from you. Because this poisons the physical body, the body starts to get older and die. Yes, the physical body in its substance is immortal from your point of view. The Bible writes about people who had lived hundreds years until they were transformed, "**circumcised**" of their abilities through manipulation of the third body gate (see the part about creation of reality). But we will not digress now.

Emotion is one of the aging factors of the human body. It is about two realities. First you lose divine energy, in fact, access to it (its quantity is endless for everyone), secondly through experiencing emotion you poison your body which then gradually dies. At a certain point the body will die completely.

So, if you understand what emotion is and how it is created, we can move to another technique called non-fighting. To the divine power of presence.

The most important factor is your ability to realize that emotion is coming. This you have to live, train and realize at all times.

In the beginning use consistency. Do not evaluate what you are doing well or wrong. Do not judge. Practice consistently. The difference is that you have already started on the journey. You do not only speak or dream about it, you have begun to live it. You do live it.

Immediately you will receive proof (signs), you will recognize them securely. The main thing is to practice, to observe for now. In the next chapter we will learn how to do so.

Emotion is Coming

So, how does one recognize that emotion is coming? For this we use presence. By observing its non-presence (absence).

When are you present? When you do not doubt about it. For example, you are present at the moment when you are creating something. Like a carpenter when he works with wood, when he sands it, he is fully present. You can see his focused expression. In this moment he is present, he is creating. He has the ability to create in the present moment. The presence consists of present moments. Between each of those moments is a crossroad and you are constantly making a decision whether to continue or not. Even if you divide the time (your perception of chronological = successive time, sequence of seconds, minutes, hours...) into very small segments, stretches. Each of those stages is divided from others by a crossroad of decision making. Infinitely cut into uncountable pieces it is still the same.

When are you absent? You come home and suddenly you realize that you do not know at all how you got there. Which way you drove and what happened to you during your journey. You had taken a well-known route and it went automatically. It is, of course, because you know the route safely, each canal, each light. But this is only a part of the truth. The same has happened to you even during an unknown route. On the way to your holiday destination. If you really know the route from work to home because you have been driving it every day for the past ten years, then you do not know the route through foreign countries to holidays equally in detail. Although it happens even there.

How is it that you do not know what you were doing? You were controlled by some present creature which had used you as a source of energy. Very possibly on the way you were remembering what happened in the past or you were thinking what will happen in the future. In any case it means that you were not present. Do you realize what could have happened? You could have crashed, ran over somebody or anything else. Why did not this happen? Because the present creature which attacked you was satisfied with your co-operation. So, the present creature took you home, safely. Safely for now. As we said, the present creatures basically lack ego and mind. At the time we will deny this statement but now thanks to it we will better learn to recognize them. So, on this trip home by car you were not present. Passing drivers saw your absent expression. Maybe you yourself have sometimes noticed the same thing. You saw a man with an absent expression behind the steering wheel, maybe he was even looking elsewhere than where he was driving.

Using the examples of the carpenter in the workshop and the absent driver (maybe also a carpenter) we have shown how they drive home. One human being in the two cases. When he is himself and creates, he is divine. Also when he is a manipulated puppet. I will emphasize the second aspect with the case when the carpenter is lying in bed and remembering the quarrel with his boss (for example like with the owner of the workshop). So, you have the entire picture.

How to remain in the present? To realize presence. As soon as you realize presence itself, it will no longer be only a term or time period for you. For that we will use the power hidden in the cross and the power (information) hidden in the Smaragdine Table. Now the cross will be turned as the capital "X". This principle is also used in your body. The left hemisphere controls the right part of the body and vice versa. The picture projected in the eye is crossed and is also transferred cross wise to the opposite half of the brain. Muscle fibres cross. Yes, you start to understand. We are working with the principles as old as this reality itself, with the principles of creation. We are dealing with ourselves. In the same way as Jesus knew the principles and applied them. I am writing it simply for easier understanding, grasping.

We will explain the words: "understand and grasp". First we will describe "to grasp the problem" – it is about ownership. If I grasp something, then I have it, I own it. It has become a part of myself. This is very important. Either if we deal with a kind of information or – beware – if we deal with material things. This connection in fact appears also in relation to tangible things. They may become a part of yourself. If you attach yourself to something in this way, it becomes you, a part of yourself. You can easily observe this with a child who has become unusually attached to a particular toy and cries a lot if he loses it. No other toy, even one of a better quality can replace it. This is because it is not about a particular type of toy but about the concrete toy that had become a part of the child.

Another word "to understand" means in fact "to under-stand". Under = to be under (something) and stand = to stand (be in certain a position). If you "understand" something, then in fact your mind understands it. This something is then accepted by the mind and the mind is not in opposition, it is in unity and does not obstruct with its doubts, questions and other things. So, if I understand something, then I stand under the mind, I am in its power but not under its reign and I can also use its power. I am in the space of the mind's acceptance. If I understand something I am in harmony with this something. This will later enable us to create reality.

Be aware of outspoken principles and use your divine power and energy for yourself. You already know that the path goes through presence. So, through the "Son" (Jesus). Nor through the past, "Father", neither through the future, through the "Holy Spirit", that has not yet been realized in tangible reality and does not exist from the material point of view. Again I am using religious terminology. For simplicity.

You may better know the description: "Salvation through Jesus Christs". Purposely I have not yet used this phrase. Now we will clarify it. It is the emphasis of the presence. Placing presence in the middle of the cross of space and time. Jesus of Nazareth (presence) placed at the cross (the symbol of decision, the crossroad). So that, the symbol is in the symbol.

Only through the presence do you have the possibility to be free. Now we will clarify how to achieve it.

"To clarify" means to shed light on it, to illuminate it. We will bring it to divine light.

You have already started to observe your emotions. To realize them. For example, when you get angry with your children because they have been naughty. In the chapter about children you will understand why this previous sentence is nonsense. But now we will use it to explain what we need.

At the latest, after you have let emotion influence you, after you have yelled it all out, realize what has happened. You allowed someone to drain you of your energy. It is not important who it was. We will not be dealing with that for a moment, it would distract you unnecessarily. What happened is that you got angry. For sure you were mean during that incident. This will make you feel sorry later on. The present creature has "deposited into the bank" part of your energy in the form of feelings from which it may create emotion whenever. In the same way that we describe.

You do not say "become angry", but we say "get angry" which means that you are not angry but you are getting this evil – anger from the outside, from the place out of you, yourself. In this case it is clear (possible) not to accept this and not to become bad – not to get this evil (get angry). To remain yourself. So, if you get angry, then you got something from the outside, this something had caused emotion. Realize that you were then controlled by emotions. Do not look for either causes nor consequences. Only realize that you have become a victim of emotion. So, something or somebody had been actively abusing you.

The Phase of Realizing the Presence

This is the first phase of how to consciously become present; by realizing that you have been controlled. You are sitting on your bed, out of breath (thinking about the story with your boss) or you are walking around the room with a cigarette. You are wiping away your tears after a touching movie. You are shocked while watching the TV news where teenagers had tortured a cat to death or where a father had raped his daughter. Everyone is affected by different things. Some topics work on a bigger group of people. These are yet "unmilked" topics. A gun-fight between the mafia and the police would probably not surprise us. The same applies to a murder somewhere in a dark forest. Nothing will come out of this. There are more interesting topics and you will see how they will multiply.

I have described how the first phase of realizing work with emotions has proceeded. It is about realizing, right after you had experienced emotion, that it happened. Nothing more. It's enough for now. By the time you start to practice it, you will see that it is not such a simple task as it seemed to you at the beginning.

The next phase is to realize that you have been controlled. This is the state when you are running across the factory hall and yelling that somebody has taken your tools. Or you may be yelling at your children because they have broken something once again.

If you realize emotion already in this phase, you are a step further. You perceive emotion when it is affecting you. Its power is weakened by this. Why? Because you are getting yourself to a state very close to presence.

Darkness (emotion) may not exist in the presence of light (your conscious presence in the process)! The more often you are present the less emotion can control you. This is true. This explanation should be enough for this phase.

In this way you will begin to observe the emotions which you have already experienced or in a better scenario (maybe later), emotion which happens right in the moment.

Through this work on yourself, you will move to a point where it really is about something. As I have already said and as you certainly know, it is about the soul. Nothing less.

I Cannot Recognize Emotion When It Is Coming. What Should I Do?

Some emotions are easily recognizable and controllable. Some are much more difficult and their attack is more sophisticated.

If you have already reached the phase in which you recognize that you have been attacked, that you had experienced emotion, you definitely have an idea of how difficult it will be to get some of them under control. With easier emotions like anger you can probably imagine that you will be able to deal with them. But there are other emotions, such as fear where it will be more difficult. I wish I could say otherwise but it is exactly like that.

We will start with the easier one. The story of your boss. If you are sitting on your bed and you might have an accelerated pulse, then realize what has happened and what you have experienced. If you already have more practical experience, you will realize what is happening already in the moment when you are watching the projection of ego and mind.

The result which is necessary to reach is to recognize **incoming** emotion. To recognize emotion before you start to experience it.

It is not possible to do it without practical experience. You have to immediately implement each piece of information you read in this book into your life. Either as a trial or to prove to me (or to yourself) that it is not true. Later it will not even matter what the first reason was. You, yourself are what really matters. Just try it and keep trying. Take my word for it. This is the only way how to reach the transformation of consciousness. By only reading and philosophizing in the manner of "hmm, I have read this somewhere and it doesn't really work" won't get you anywhere.

If I say how and what to observe, then do it. You will see that there are stranger things around you than in some sci-fi movie. If you allow me I will take you out of the "System". You will not live by someone else's judgement of you. You will live yourself. You will be free.

In our story of the argument with the boss, try to realize how everything happened. For this, take advantage of your extra sensory skills. You don't have to be afraid that you don't have them. The fact that you don't realize them does not mean that you don't have them. If you are a woman this is especially true.

We Are Beginning to Activate
Extra Sensory Perception

How do you then use your extra sensory perception? Again, it is about using some of the divine principles we have mentioned before. Try to imagine the process backwards. You start by incidentally activating this way of perceiving because you will activate parts of the brain which have been used less up to now.

In the evening go through everything you have experienced during the day. But be careful, not from the morning – start from now and go back to when you first woke up. In the beginning this will be quite difficult – to keep focused, especially for men. You will see how many blank spaces there will be on the map. Places where you were completely absent. Try it but don't make dogma out of this practice. There are more levels that you will gradually discover. With this method you may recall for example an experience that might have otherwise been overlooked.

This will be more difficult for men. This is because men use their brains differently than women. The brain is the tangible organ of mind. The mind is located in two areas of the brain, but mind itself is divided into three parts. The third part is in the area called the solar plexus. Because you imagine the process backwards, you involve mind differently. It goes both from the back and from the front at the same time. Also, the female principle is in play and therefore there is a certain balance. The big (front) brain is divided into two parts – the left side and the right side. The way in which you use your brain determines which part of brain is used most of the time.

Simply said, by using one part of the brain you recollect the process from the back and the other part from the front. If it goes well, then it is because of the harmony of both its parts. If mind is, let's say in unity from two thirds (2/3), then we can better reach harmony of mind and soul. This is the presumption for being present. You already recognize the power of the presence. Now realize how much remains for the complete harmony of the three substances of a human being. What power you will possibly gain by that...

In the story of the boss it is the same. We will try to go through the process together. We will start after you experienced emotion when you are sitting on your bed or on the balcony smoking a cigarette, your pulse is accelerated and you feel miserable. You are trying to find your lost calm. We will go further (nearer). You are lying in bed, you have an absent expression (for the observer) and you are watching the movie shown by "someone" in your head. In this movie you are standing opposite your boss and you are trying to defend yourself. Maybe you are only suffering silently, you have no chance to say anything. Anger and despair accumulate inside you. In this phase the flow of energy is the most obvious, therefore we will stop here for a moment.

The Voice in Your Head

You also perceive a voice in your head. It might be more understandable for you if I would say that you perceive a thought which is taking place. I am purposely not using this definition. It really is the voice in your head. Why? Because the voice pronounces words. The word has divine power. The word creates. If the voice pronounces something, it has the energy of creation. So, you have to deal with it, react to it. Maybe you will recognize these words after repeated reading (in another place). What voice is this about? I will show this to you right away. Find a book somewhere in your surrounnings on which something is written, anything at all. You can also use a bottle of water or wine on the table. We need any written text, words. Now read them quietly, without speaking.

And this is the voice.

It is the voice of your ego.

Try it several times. Realize that if you look at the writing on the bottle you know without reading what is written there. The one who reads and pronounces it is ego. You don't have the need to read it for yourself – to repeat what you already know. The one who does that is ego. It is in fact a judgment, ego's attitude. It's the same as if you look at some person. You only have one look and at that moment you know everything about him. But because you say: "Oh, look at that," you are making a judgment. Respectively, your ego is making a judgment. And because you allow ego to pronounce this, even you are making a judgment.

This is very important to realize. Pay proper attention to it. This is the voice I will be describing further.

Exactly with this voice your ego says to you: "Careful, he is making a fool of you!" – "But he cannot fool you,

you're a university graduate." – "You are so well read, he will not catch you on that."

Now we will finish the reverse process of realizing of what has happened when emotion was experienced in the story of the argument with the boss. We are at the stage when you are watching the process – the argument. During this time you experience the following moments. Your ego reacts to the words that your boss is saying and which, according to you, offend or humiliate you. You realize this because you ego says: "Be careful! He is insulting you. He did it again. You cannot let him walk all over you. What will he think of you if you let him do that? What will he do next time?"

These words activate your mind. Mind immediately comes up with strategies and reactions. Either direct rewards or revenge later on if fear does not allow an immediate reaction. It does not matter much what the argument was about. It is now about the personal insult to you (your ego) by your boss (very probably by his ego). You cannot think of anything else but how to pay him back, how to hurt him. To prove to him, to everybody (to yourself?) that he is not right, that you are right. You want satisfaction. At any cost. So that he knows how you feel because of him. You are fully under the power of ego and ego enjoys its actual reign a lot. It gains energy from you and stores it in the form of reserve. These reserves have labels and ego can use them at the "right" (convenient) time.

So, this is what happens right at the moment when your boss criticizes you or gives you a warning. Ego tells you that it is an attack. The same applies with a marital quarrel and so on.

To make you believe and to make mind believe, ego plays many other movies simultaneously to you at a subconscious level which you are not aware of. In fact, it is difficult for you to even realize the movie being played in your consciousness. The one we are talking about now. The other movies are connected to your experiences. Some time ago mystics had thought that it was a separate entity. But be aware that it is the deeper art of ego which is more and more powerful and interconnected with other present creatures that influence your life situation, this reality.

You are just a spectator for now. In the best case scenario. If you allow this possibility, then let me to push a bit more. If you are in a real situation (which mind is watching only as a spectator of a movie about a real situation), during the conversation with your boss, then reason (power, thanks to which ego has such control over you) is hidden in the movies played in the subconscious at that moment. You cannot realize these movies yet. You can identify them as weird feelings at best. Something like an ancient curse. A feeling of a bygone betrayal. Simply a feeling. That is why mind believes ego so easily that it is being attacked and reacts the same way as if watching a movie at a conscious level. So in bed it is the same "trick" which is very simple and very effective.

This is already very close to the current awareness of the state of reality. Of the creatures which inhabit this reality together with us and about its practices and the aims they want to reach by using them...

Short Summary

I have described emotion as a toxin which poisons your body. From a tangible point of view it can even kill you. More precisely said it can deprive the physical body. Emotion is an allergic reaction to the mind. Present creatures live from your energy which is released when emotion is experienced. Emotion arises from a movie projected by a present creature in your consciousness. This movie is watched by mind in cooperation with ego. At the moment when mind is convinced (believes) that it is watching a real action (it identifies itself with the projected movie), it gives this information to the body. The body reacts as if it was a real action but because it knows it is not, it reacts with something more – with an allergic reaction. This is a reaction to something that the body cannot stand. The body is a physical, tangible and therefore it cannot accept movement in existence without necessary successive time – a certain time period that everything has to last for. The body cannot identify itself with unreal situations (unreal in this present moment). Existence roblems occur and the body produces energy – emotion. It is a bit more complicated to explain and we will touch upon this topic again in the part about creation of reality. Now it is important to realize what has happened. Ego got what it wanted.

The Reverse Movement of Action

Let's continue in reverse movement of the process of experiencing emotion. We stopped at the moment in which you realized that you were experiencing emotion. Let us go further. You find yourself in a state of disturbance. What was before? Now we get to the main part of the whole theme – to the beginning of emotion. How did it all start?

You are lying in bed and something has attacked you.

Now you know what it was and how it further displayed itself. You can realize when it is over. You can realize when it is happening. The question remains, how did it start?

We have already decoded this sentence. That is the key. How did it attack you? In the most elemental way. The way which is described in the first book of Moses, Genesis.

It attacked you by **WORD**. Not by a thought, but by word. This has very often been confused – it is very simple to confuse it – without the ability to realize facts and connections.

Remember reading the label on the bottle. What is it? This something that you hear in your head while you are reading? A thought? No, words! Words that someone pronounces. Who? A present creature that is getting ready to control you and take away a part of your energy.

If we go deeper, then the primary thing which had started a further process, was the word. At the moment when you meet your boss the first thing which had sounded in your head, which someone (ego) cried out was, for example, "What does he want now?" or "Look at the face he is making at you". Maybe even some more sentences ran through your head before the boss actually did say something. As soon as he started speaking it was then clear to you what was about to happen next.

Now, the important moment for us is when a chain of events is started which at the end is the experienced emotion. The answer is: **"It is triggered by words pronounced by a present creature."** Mind reacts to the words and the process gets moving. The complete truth is even a bit more complicated. Simply said, the word is pronounced by ego which is under the control of present creatures.

Did an analogy of formula with the pronouncement of magic words cross your mind? It is like that. The process described above and its clarification is very simple. Surely you understand that to describe the whole process in detail right at the beginning would be intolerable for many of you. Intangible energies enter this action, present creatures have cooperated (or fought) with each other already for a long time. Relationships are difficult and trigger more sophisticated mechanisms. Everything is connected with everything else.

Right now we are at the threshold of understanding and realizing a basic ancient principle. This principle is so original that even the Bible – The Old Testament in its first book, mentions the use of this "magic" instrument of god as one of the first events. It is about the word.

In connection with the word I will give another example of its power. An example which is connected with you more than you may want to admit now. It is the theme of fairies, fortune tellers, horoscopes and the like.

What information from tales do we keep for ourselves? I'm talking about fortune tellers. If someone tells you something at the moment when you have a pure consciousness, like that of a child, those words will influence you for many years, maybe for your whole life. Do not let anyone talk to your children. That does not mean to isolate them from the world. Only be careful what somebody might say to them. Immediately clarify nonsense and manipulation they might hear.

This is the same when you are being like a child who believes anything asking a fortune teller about your future or trying to find answers from astrologers. The predictions do not come true because they are true, but because you believe in them. You will realize this yourself especially through recognizing the possibilities of how to create your own part of reality.

In this moment I am speaking about it in connection with the power of the word. Because exactly by this power (and usually only by this power) false prophets come into control...

Before we start dealing with the technique of how not to "fall into" a trap set by a present creature, it is necessary to go back to some terms that have already been mentioned, but not clarified.

Intangible and Tangible

For those of you who do not orientate yourselves easily in these expressions, I will briefly explain them. Existence – space, being or however you would call the world in which you are in, has many explanations of its creation, what it consists of and of mutual relationships. It depends on whether you look into a scientific publication or to a religious text. Advocates of both sides have greatly different opinions. Where does the truth lie? Allow me the following simple description.

Try to imagine that you are a flea and you are looking at a car. From your point of view. With the knowledge in your mind that you now attribute to a flea. What does the flea possibly think about the car when it looks at it from the front? It can describe the car – in its own words. It can see the lights, the front window, etc. If it has a good position, it can even see inside the car. Another flea is looking from the side. Another one from the back, from above and from below to the car chassis. Another got inside and browsed through the interior. Another one is in the engine block. I could go on and on. I'm sure you are starting to see where I'm going with this. The fleas will get together and describe to each other what they have seen. Each of them is convinced of its own truth – after all, the flea is really describing what it has seen and experienced. Their opinions are different. The one which was in the engine area doesn't understand what lights the other fleas are talking about. Especially if they cannot even agree with each other. The one which was in the front has a completely different description than the one which was in the back. The flea which had watched the car from above does not believe that the car has wheels. It has seen the car and knows for sure that it does not have wheels. You will not convince it otherwise.

It is true that this is a very simple example. Do you see how difficult is to accept a different point of view? What prevents the fleas from acknowledging another extent of the truth? Why do not they move a bit further? Ego and mind prevent them from doing so. Mind knows what it can see. Ego supports mind in the opinion that the others want to make fool of it. Arguments fly in the air, the discussion turns into a disagreement and it isn't about the car anymore but about something else, about ego. Other present creatures come and drain the energy which fleas (people) flash around. The fleas argue and then go their separate ways. Each has its own truth which truly matches their reality.

The same goes with opinions about the universe. Different groups of people agree with each other about some things but sharply disagree about others. But in fact it would be enough to walk a little bit and look at it from another point of view. Different present creatures obstruct this.

We will now describe the expressions "intangible" and "tangible". They are quite understandable and acceptable for the mind. The expression tangible describes the physical perception of the world. Intangible describes the metaphysical. So, everything what stands behind, out of this material world that most of all science (with its proof) claims to clarify. The intangible world is claimed by esoterica, religion and others. Why are those expressions suitable for mind? It is (of course) in words. Both words consist of the word "tang" which means to touch in Latin. The mind knows this word and can identify itself with it, understands it and has already verified it. Yes, mass really exists. These words describe the ease of perception – touch. The mind knows that it is easier to perceive what can be touched.

Now understand intangible as to tactual and invisible and tangible as visible and touchable (recognizable through the five human senses).

Present Creatures

This is what I generally call each entity which comes into contact with human beings, respectively with your own being (soul), in any way. The substance of present creatures is different and we can say that almost all descriptions available in esoteric books are right in their own way. The evolution of these entities is as old as this reality itself. At different times they fulfilled various functions and tasks. Sometimes they disaffiliated themselves or transformed to another dimensions. They were sometimes called gods and realized themselves here on the Earth. There are many stories about them. The most important thing for you now is (only) a basic understanding. Present creatures are energy-information entities. "Energy" because they work with energy and their "bodies" are partly created by energy. They exist by the rules of the intangible – metaphysical world. "Information" because they contain certain information about this reality (some principles). "Energy" = potential (appetite, ability), "information" = the way, know-how. You will first succeed in communicating with mind, which is a very interesting entity that is a part of the human being (more precisely said – a part of the physical body). Mind is connected both with tangible reality and partly (from its substance) with intangible reality. We can say that mind stands at the border of the intangible and the tangible reality, similarly to man himself.

Present creatures, energy-information entities, have an energy part which (for simplification) creates their "body" and as you will recognize further, creates their potential, the male principle. Then they have an information part which creates their inspiration, the female principle. This is very worthwhile information. By realizing this information you will gain very unconventional skills. Extra sensory skills. You will be able to realize facts and connections and to differentiate between facts and hypothesis.

The present creature has one quality that will be for you (for your ego) difficult to accept and understand at first sight. It is the ability to move in space (also in time, if you wish). Because it exists (functions) on different principles which we will only be discovering later, some "miraculous" appearances are quite normal for it. The skills you may admire about other people, that they can read thoughts, move objects and so on, are for a present creature the same skills that for example breathing for you. They are capable of doing even more. For us, it is now important to realize that here with us there are beings more powerful than some would like to admit.

A few mystics and not only of this time, have anticipated the existence of these creatures. Thanks to their high level of consciousness and courage, some have even started to observe them and describe them. There have always been human beings here who were even able to communicate with them. You will also be able to do so. It is only necessary to practice and to have a certain level of consciousness.

I have named them "present creatures" because their power is connected with the power of the present moment. Also, because they are present at all decisions and at all crossroads of your being.

They are simply present and therefore very powerful. It is necessary to deal with them with respect and at eye level.

The Mind

The mind is one of the intangible parts of a human being. The human being is a trinitarian being inseparably consisting of the physical body, the soul (the own being) and the spirit. The mind is a part of the body and in this way it is also partly realized in tangible reality, as the human brain. Intangibly, the mind is situated in the area of the head as well as in the area of the body (the solar plexus).

The mind is an allied entity. I say this even though (or right because) I seemingly deny this statement.

The mind is your mentor in "earthly matters", tangible matters. It is the leading drafter of science. Here, and in connection with what has been said, I will clarify another divine principle, power, an art which you will learn to control. If you need to communicate with anyone, always do so at eye level. Do not look at anyone or anything from above and do not lower yourself to anything or anyone. It is the only fair way of negotiation and communication. **Communication should be done at eye level.** This is another mystery, another message of divine power. Your knowledge will be richer and it is good idea to lay this book down from time to time or to read some parts over.

From a tangible point of view, the mind is found in the brain. Above the level of the eyes. This is the main reason (cause) why the mind had started to override the soul. Do you know the saying of how "eyes are the window to the soul"? Eyes really have another meaning apart from being a tangible organ of sensory perception. They are the part of the physical body that gets older differently than the rest. You can observe "young eyes" on old people. This is related to their soul. The eyes are directly connected to the soul, which is immortal. One eye represents the female aspect and the other, the male aspect. They can even be of different sizes. A human's face shows his "inner" picture. Face = form. The face has been formed and bent by inner processes which stay written on the face. What is inside is the same as what appears outside.

Exactly because of this placement (above the eye level) the mind started to think that it stood above the own being. It had started to demand the final word in decision making. Pay attention here to the expression "final word". Again, the hidden truth in what we normally know and use, is being brought to light: to have **the final word**. In the moment when the mind fully present conscious said for the first time: "I now have the final word". It had given rise to the understanding of time and a new dimension of ego.

The mind, on the basis of its existence in the area above the eye level, had taken over most of decision-making powers of the human being. Here we are, from a consecutive time point of view hundreds of thousands years in the past. The Mind had separated itself from the body and set itself as an independent present creature. How is this possible? We have already said that it is possible to create in presence using divine energy. Human beings contain divine energy and the ability to create. Whatever originated from human beings has the same abilities at the deepest level. So, also the Mind, before a part of a human being, could have worked (created), if it was able to realize it, with these principles. What happened was that the Mind had taken over the reign. It had started to play this "game", but with your figurine. Probably in this moment most present creatures had appeared, arisen including present creatures like Fear or Death. With this concept understand the Mind like "a super creature". Something which arose over the mind in the way that you have understood it until this point. More precisely said, it separated itself, created a new, another Mind which felt itself to be an independent creature outside the human being.

The Mind is a very powerful instrument and an admirable creature in its precision and consistency, which has achieved the creation of wonderful tangible things. The more it created, the more it was sure about its "mission", its determination of the one who has the final word. This is the history of the present time.

The mind always has the edge, it is placed above eye level. It looks at everything and everyone from above. During the time which it has existed this way, the Mind has created all branches of science and human knowledge, science itself. It has let come into being many self-feeding present creatures which prey (free-load) on human beings. One example for everything. Inseparable couples – illness and medicine. Only a few know that under the blanket of cognition, the Mind dissected the human body. In fact it was searching for what it had lost when it split from the body, it was searching for itself. Integrity. The Mind is missing something, itself. This is why the separated Mind (super-creature) has not succeeded and will not succeed in fully understanding the brain...

During the last several hundred years the Mind has promoted itself to be the ruler of almost everything. In the past there were not so many human beings isolated from the intangible part of reality. From a certain, but inaccurate (purposeful) point of view there were not so many human beings without faith. Thanks to the Mind, dissociation of human beings has occurred. The Mind continues to push and examine further. What pushes the Mind though? What kind of engine does it run on? Ego? No, not this time. It is Fear. Again, Fear as a super-creature, the superstructure of fear as a feeling.

The Mind during it's creation (achieving independence) let come into being or created for its own needs many creatures which later on got out of its control. An analogy with the current political world is offered when one super-power educates, trains and arms warriors against another power and at the end is destroyed by them. It is the same with the Mind.

The mind is a present entity and at the same time a part of the human being which it knows but does not realize. These are some of the signs of the coming chaos. The Mind is now at the peak of its being as an independent creature. Your task is to start communicating with it, put it back in its place. Although in the beginning there will be several problems, the mind is interested and you need the mind for realization. Again, it is an allied entity.

Considering that the Mind has the final word at the moment, we will deal with it in detail already now.

From where does the Mind get so much energy for its reign? We have said that it is from Fear. Nowadays, it is one of the most powerful creatures of this reality. How it gets this energy you can see in the second part of this book where I deal with the creation of reality. Briefly, I can describe it such that the frequency of the mind is either fear or faith. Both of them make the accessible (open) to the flow of energy.

If I wrote that the Mind takes energy from Fear, then fear (a feeling) is the one that controls the mind (a part of the body).

Let's go back to the mind. How to now perceive this (the mind) for the purpose of transformation of consciousness. The mind as a present entity is the first one with which you will learn to communicate. **To communicate means first of all, to listen and the path leads this way.** The same with emotions – first you will manage to see the emotion after it is already gone, then when it is affecting you and so on. The same when you will be communicating with the mind, first you will only be listening. That does not mean you have to obey each of its word. Just listen, more precisely said, perceive its opinions, attitudes etc. This way you will manage to get in touch. You will use the divine power I have described before. Communication at eye level. The mind is not a subordinate that should serve you. At the same time, the Mind is neither your god. Now, in this moment it stops telling you what to do. It is not its business. The mind has an advisory voice. You have the deciding word.

Let us stop for a while at the term "to perceive at eye level". As in other divine principles, great strength and power is hidden in this. Spend some time in understanding this statement.

If you should identify the most important part of the human body, would it be the brain that controls everything? Would it be the heart which pumps needed oxygen? Would it be the lungs which gain this oxygen? Would it be the mouth or the nose through which we breathe? We could continue like this on and on. In the end, you would discover that everything in the human body is "the most" important at the same level. If one part leaves, it is not possible for the rest to go on. Therefore it is not necessary to make up any hierarchies, to highlight or to overlook something. This is the work (manner) of the Mind.

This is also a part of the meaning of the statement, acting at eye level. **You need everything what your body consists of, what your body is.** You need this all equally. Therefore, it is not possible to differentiate between the more important and the less important. Evaluation is connected with this and also the approach to everything. If you have people, things, needs and anything else that you can think of, divided into better and worse, needed and less needed, then you should leave this attitude as soon as possible. What attitude? The position of a judge, what else is this in fact.

One wise judge answered the question if his statement was just by these words: "I am dealing with submitted facts and I am bound by the law. I am only a judge. Justice? You can only look to God for that."

Free yourself of the attitude of judging all that surrounds you, even yourself. Perceive everything to be equally important and needed equally because that's the way it really is. Perceive everything at eye level. At the same level as you perceive yourself. This is an important presumption for extra sensory perception and especially for inner harmony. Without this, happiness or freedom are not achievable.

Therefore, disharmony in perception occurs. There are many factors which we will be dealing with step by step. First of all, it is about the mind and its understanding of the world. The mind builds and pulls down pedestals, yearns and is afraid. Your objective is to grasp the mind and take it back to eye level with yourself.

Ego

Ego is another present entity closely connected with a human being. As is the mind, ego is present in human beings. It is an intangible entity. As the mind presents, in a certain sense, a "communication" aid between the body and surroundings, the ego (the own ego) presents a communication aid of the own being (soul) and the mind. It is quite complex to understand but it is not possible to simplify it any further. I am already making certain inaccuracies.

If the mind is a creature taking part in decision making, then the ego is a source of motivation (inspiration) and potential at the same time. Similarly, as the mind is connected with the body, the ego is connected with the own being.

Not even the ego is an enemy. As fully conscious enlightened beings, without ego we would exist motionless in the space of existence. Ego is what gives us an appetite for realization and living, it gives us inspiration. This is how I would describe ego at the basic level of human beings. Mutated Egos standing above this ego have different tasks that are not so friendly to you.

First of all, we will say something about the ego at the basic level, about the ego itself. The same as the mind, the ego is also afraid. Egos' manifestations are easily recognizable. It shows something to the mind all the time and pushes it to react. Ego needs to differentiate itself. In any way. Whether it be the best or the worst. If it does not succeed in occupying such a position, it then pretends to be indifferent. **Indifference is a manifestation of ego**. Ego is not an enemy. Thanks to its influence you have the appetite to do something. This is exactly its mission. But if this impulse overgrows into dictating devices, limits and aims, then it is only a blind alley of the higher Ego.

Ego is the one who insinuates that you have to take some kind of position. Obviously, you have to take a stand somewhere, be on someone's side. To be in opposition, otherwise you won't have your own opinion and that is to be punished. For that matter, it is the same if you have one. Ego is constantly ringing the alarm: "Be alert! Watch out, someone wants to cheat you or make fun of you. He only wants your money! What was the meaning of that comment? Why are they looking at me like that? Do you see that couple – they're most likely gossiping about you." Ego will not forgive the slightest deviation from the norm, even though its charge is about being different. Ego is confused, scared, and doesn't know what to believe. It says to you: "You are too short. You are ugly. You don't run fast. You can't make up your mind. You aren't very talented. Your breasts are too small. You have an ugly nose. You have a big bum." It bombards you with its fears all the time. The fear of not being accepted. The fear of losing integrity. Deep down it knows where it belongs but it is confused. What should it believe in? It wants to be different but is afraid to. It is not satisfied or happy. It starts to look for the guilty one. Who can be blamed that it (ego) cannot express itself enough? Ego starts to search and bumps into other egos which are also afraid and also searching. It starts to compare itself. It does not operate with real facts but with ideas. A battle is taking place inside. Who is better, she or me? It activates the mind immediately. It wants answers. The mind is coldly comparing – debits and credits – the first results won't take long. She is better. She has longer hair, prettier eyes and smoother skin. On what basis is it possible to pronounce such a result? On the basis of generally held norms, of course. An outgrowth of other frightened minds supported by their own egos. Other processes start running. The mind gives this information not only to ego, which asked, but also to the physical body. The body starts to react allergically. Emotion occurs. The body will not bear the poison in the form of the minds' and egos' doubts of its perfection (perfection of the physical body). The body is perfect, it knows that. The body is God's creation. It is not necessary to judge it or to circumcise it. It does not have a problem with perceiving itself. If it is free. So, what about the mind's and ego's doubts? Where do they come from?

These are the doubts from the past and begin with the doubts (fears) of your parents about your perfection – "normality".

The physical body is attacked. It starts to weaken and apart from vibrations, energy that it releases as a result of running emotion (self pity), other forms of energy are released. The body literally tears itself to pieces. Surely you know the statement "It tears (breaks) my heart." The body gets into an odd state. It creates another "body", something like a print of the physical one, but at another frequency (level) of being. This other body is not physical, tangible. It is the body compound of emotions, concrete emotions which are connected with the mind's and ego's perception of the physical body. This body is as if it's around the physical body. It is not an aura, although it can look like that way. It is another shell. But frequencies, which the physical body had displaced from itself, stick like a magnet around it. This body, because it is created by divine energy, may gradually start to disaffiliate itself. It can gain qualities and abilities similar to human beings in some aspect. Even the ego may appear. These processes are simple in substance. As if in a vacuum, elements appear and disappear, whether science admits this or not. These elements "behave" differently if watched only by an automatic camera or if watched by a living man...

Gradually, we will return to the basic part of the transformation of consciousness without which we could have gotten lost in terms and descriptions (creations of the mind). In the end it would only end up as theoretical information. You don't need this. You have already heard and read enough.

Regarding the above mentioned I will only add that through this process an affect, called by psychiatrists "schizophrenia", arises (this is one possibility of its origin). The division of personality. It is more complicated but these are the principles. In your everyday practice you can notice these "other" bodies on other people. You don't need anything for it, just your own perception. I am sure you have already met at some point in your life a person who was extremely unlikeable to you, without him saying or doing anything in particular. It was enough that he came into the room and the atmosphere changed very quickly. Such a person is full of stored feelings and emotions. This is one of the possible effects of what I have previously described.

Ego is a present entity which has a fundamental influence on your physical body. We will be using this information in connection with the creation of reality.

I will only add that there is a potential for discrepancy in your understanding of ego (eventually of the mind) because human beings can be controlled via these entities. Present creatures, if they want to control you, can do it directly through your ego or your mind because they are your intangible "representatives". Therefore, everything that influences and controls you, we call the ego or the mind in the end. Although, they are not the authors of a given decision, but only the ones who realize them.

The Word

We have already touched upon this topic several times directly in the text. I will give a few examples of how to comprehend and understand the word.

There will be simple clarifications. Illumination (clarification) is in fact a consecration, disappearance of the dark, shadows (doubts, ignorance, unconsciousness) through the arrival of light. Illumination – enlightenment. To light something "so that it will be well visible". Simplicity, free of many spirits, many gods, many meanings and descriptions, free from the need of vast knowledge. Simple enlightenment is that with one-single meaning, with one-single spirit, with one-single god.

A lot of thinking will not be needed for understanding. Understanding, grasping, owning something in the sense that you identify yourself with, becomes a part of you.

Thinking over and over = a conflict, a struggle of thinking, is a dispute (discrepancy) of thinking.

The word has power because it is outspoken in presence. You cannot pronounce a word in the past or in the future. Although we are talking about the future, we are pronouncing the words now, in the present. **Each moment is in fact presence, only at a different place of existence.** From this, the relativity of time arises. Its existence is impossible to deny. But the common understanding of time is very different from the truth.

When I say "imagine", it means to put an image before the actual presence. Make it real (present) in conceptions (inside). Make it real – realize it, make it present, that place in existence. Move in space to the place where exists in presence that what I now want you to see (sense) and imagine. Imagine in spirit that…

What does **in spirit** mean? You are familiar with this. It is the same as imagining yourself. Why then in spirit? It is in cooperation with God, you are using divine energy. A spirit as "the most divine" part of the human being, realizing power, enters into this co-operation.

Again, I will not be able to avoid comparisons with religion. Do not understand God here as God (the Holy Father), God the way he is presented to children, a wise old man on a little cloud in heaven. Perceive God here according to the Holy Trinity, as the Son, as we have said, as the Presence. This statement is in the sense of presence. The spirit, here as a part of a human being (trinitarian), represents the substance of spirit, the connection with God.

You have always known what "imagine in spirit" means. Now you know what it really means and how it works. We

77

will get to the point of how it works precisely a bit later. For the time being you have been collecting necessary information, before we move on to the practical exercises of how to adopt the skills. Exactly in this way it is possible to change reality.

I have mentioned the cross, its center, as the symbol of the presence. But where does one find the cross in connection with the word? We have said that the principle of crossing is applied into this reality (wrongly interpreted as the system of opposites).

Many crossings occur in the human body, both on tangible and intangible levels. For simplification, we will be dealing only with the symbol itself. Where do we find it? In the area of the fifth chakra which is the centre of communication. The brain's control of the body passes right through this chakra.

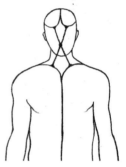

It is the area where the energy of the fifth and the sixth chakras blend. It is represented by the mouth. The power of this cross stands behind the magical kiss, which in fairy tales awakens a princess...

Jews, Christians, Muslims

Before we move on in the transformation of consciousness, we will stop for a moment at religions. Just for a while because it is important. Many predictions and prophecies have been uttered. Many of them are included right in religion.

Slowly, all outspoken curses are being consummated. We live in unsettled times and if it seems hectic to you, you are right. The Mind has been losing control. But this is only one of its images – the image of the Mind. Concerned with all this noise, outer and inner, you can miss the right moment. The present moment. The mind cares about many things but there is only one which matters. The presence.

How do we understand this? Many of you do not trust churches. No wonder. But even so, it is necessary to know at least the fundamentals of the main representatives. They are Moses, Abraham, Jesus and Muhammad. They are not the only ones who influence the lives of people on this planet, but they are the most well-known and historically embedded in our geographical lines.

Jews, Christians and Muslims. Three groups of the faithful, incompatible for some, especially if we look at the current situation in the world. Though they all believe in the same god, because Yahweh, God Our Father and Allah are one and the same. The tradition of these three religions arises from the same basis which was created in the Old Testament.

Abraham, as the forefather of all three groups was chosen by god to create the nation of Israelites (Jews). There was a land allocated to him where they should live. We will not go into much detail, we will just briefly say who is who. The Jewish line is clear, God in dealing with Abraham asked for the circumcision of all his offspring. Moses as a prophet, describes in his books the creation of the world and Abraham's doings. Jesus, also a Jew in origin, therefore an ancestor of Abraham, was also circumcised. His acting as Messiah was very controversial at the time. It is necessary to say, that in the time when Jesus was preaching his teachings, there were more of these "modern" enlighteners who did not agree with some of the dogma, the "officially" acknowledged belief.

Also Muhammad, as a successor of the ancestral line of Abraham, was circumcised. For elaboration I will add that Abraham had a son, Ismael with his slave, Hagar. This son, according to what god had said, was to also establish a nation. From this ancestral line comes Muhammad.

It is possible to say that all the main representatives of these religious directions have the same origin. At least from the mind's point of view. Why then have there been so many clashes througout history? Does it even have a religious character? The answer is simple. It is about Ego. If there would be one God, as the Old Testament and other books derived from it say, why it would create three clashing religions, which all praise him? We will not be dealing with these issues for long. I am only offering you different examples which are much bigger than what we have been dealing with in the introduction. Until now we have been dealing with the being of one man. Now, I am offering you for a little while, a view of the other end of this false hierarchy of present creatures which control human beings; a view of the part of the System, which religions are only a piece of (a certain "executive power"). As I have said, the mind is not the enemy, quite the opposite is true. Thanks to its skills of analyzing facts, a tangle of half-truths and myths will become clearer to you. Using the technique of perception which we have presented before, if I do not know what something is, I will start with what it is not. From the brief description which I gave, it is possible to deduce what the conflicts between the religions are not. They do not have a religious character because all these religions are in fact saying the same thing, just through the mouths of other (its) prophets.

If these words, more precisely said, their interpretation, would be free of Ego, then these religions would surely find some common ground (the same speech). But as we can see in the media, reality is different.

Another example which I will use is the structuring of Christian churches. It is possible to see that even the churches based on one god and his one representative (Jesus Christ) cannot find the same speech. Many of churches exist. Let us simplify them into two main streams: the Catholic Church and the Orthodox Church. Why did they arise? The simple answer is, that once again it was about Ego, about power, as usual. There was some variance in faith found by "ordinary believers" and this was interpreted as very fundamental. In times of the early medieval rulers and bishops the church had great power, even greater than the rulers of particular countries. This power was concentrated onto the church's centre, to the Pope (the primate of Rome's bishop). How to become emancipated from such influence? By establishing a new and different church, one's own, which would not be governed by a central "command". This is the origin of church's split. In the beginning particular Christian streams were certainly not united, not until the successive establishing of the "right" faith at Constantine's councils. In fact, not even after that, but at the time it had gotten a certain order. The Mind had created it at Ego's instruction.

The Mind has often intervened in religion. As the last example, I will bring the mind's influence on the creation of Christian holidays. Isn't it strange that so many holidays are very close to each other timewise in both Christian and Jewish traditions? Jewish tradition is incomparably older than Christian. How do you want to turn people around to faith and not let them have the holidays and traditions that they are used to? It is sufficient to keep the holidays, just rename them and give them another "reason", and it is done. People have their holidays. Ego has its new faith and its sheep. So, the Mind and Ego cooperate in perfect unison. I am using simple (on purpose) clarifications because it would be necessary to state all historical connections for a more comprehensive survey.

Everything has been escalating and great changes are awaiting us in the upcoming years. We will witness mysteries which do not have an equivalent in modern history. It is necessary to raise and widen our consciousness; the ability (not only knowledge) to perceive, influence and create. It is already possible to see it now. That some do not see, does not mean that there is nothing to see. When the legendary Titanic was sinking music was playing and people were dancing until the very last moment.

Some people make fun of old nations and their teachings. Other have been discovering them and are now standing up on platforms and speaking about them, as if they were familiar with them. **Beware of false prophets!**

"Because false messiahs and false prophets will appear and show signs and wanders to deceive, if possible, the elect."
Mark, 13,22

"Modern" spiritual streams have been spreading across Western countries in the past several years, such as Buddhism and streams derived from it (the Diamond Path and many others). The teachings of the Toltec, Maya and others have been appearing as well. No wonder. Current (local) religions do not offer much truth which would be simple to accept and understand. People are tired and too tied down by the church's dogma. The truth contained in messages is not complete or has been manipulated, so it has not been "fresh" for hundreds of years. "New" beliefs – streams, if you wish, offer "fresh" blazing truth and messages. **Don't forget that they do not contain anything different that we haven't already long known from the words of "local" prophets**. It isn't necessary to search for new paths and new truths. You can just open your eyes and read the truth in texts that we have had at our disposal for almost two thousand years.

How "Not to Fall" into a Set Trap

Let's now go back to dealing with ourselves, within the transformation of consciousness. I will quickly remind you of where we are.

We have described a fictitious story of a carpenter. It could be him, who experiences emotion after a conflict with his boss. With this example, I have described what processes occur. We shed light on whom and which way such processes enter. Further, we have described the particular principles of using divine power, energy. We will now start practicing the above mentioned knowledge. We are at the next phase – creating skills.

We know what emotion is, why and roughly how it arises. We also know that the whole situation in the fictitious story of the conflict with the boss began at a particular moment. It began when the mind reacted to a certain word (sentence) pronounced by a present creature, the mind in this moment identified itself with a screened movie. Whether it is at a conscious level some time in the evening while you are in bed, or in real time at the moment of the conflict, at an unconscious level.

What happened was that ego was trying to preserve its originality (distinction) and reacted "a step ahead", as if it were in the future. It reacted to the future (fictious) which (not only) for ego keeps other entities – emotional memory. Ego was offered an analogy with another, similar situation that happened – took place somewhere in the past, maybe to someone else. This situation was chosen from the database to which an individual's emotional memory has an access. It is the database of family, race, nationality, religion etc. Now we are at a deeper level of consciousness. We are shedding light on the basis of which some present creatures act. You can see that in fact, they are also controlled and manipulated by someone else. Present creatures, like ego, are a part of you. Do not blame ego because it very often does not know what it is doing. It is under pressure from other present creatures (higher – super creatures) which control you via your mind and your ego, your intangible parts.

Ego had then initiated another process. It felt threatened because it had received some information which sounded like: "defend yourself". Ego reacted immediately. The voice in your head said something like: "the boss is attacking you". In this moment the mind was activated as a mediator between the tangible (physical) and intangible world. Ego had "screened" a short movie to the mind. The movie contained information which ego had received via emotional memory. The mind transmitted this information to the body. Emotion has arisen.

An attentive reader will now object and think, yes, but we are now in presence, at least considering what is happening. The mind does not react to what happened in the past, as if you were in bed in the evening. So, why does emotion arise?

It is the way that the mind reacts to information from ego. The same way it has reacted in the evening to information from ego, let's say, to information commented on by ego (sounded by ego's voice). So, the mind reacts to something what is not really in presence. The fact, that ego has the feeling that it will be (with the highest certainty based on previous experience) attacked, is not reality – a process that is taking place just now in the present moment. It is one potential option of the future, one of many (infinitely many) options. It is not the present moment. The movie showed to the mind does not correspond to the present moment which is just taking place. Ego's hypothesis is that it will (definitely) happen. Ego pretends (shows the movie) that it is in fact, already happening. This is the trigger mechanism of emotion. The mind hands over the information to the physical body (with which it is connected) and the body reacts according to the pattern of emotions that we already know.

Let's go even deeper. Let us slow down time, like in the movies and enlighten more delicate and less perceivable processes. For simplicity (and for finality in a sense) of clarification, let us enter the action in the moment when you are standing in front of your boss. The picture is still. Let us press the button on a fictitious player and start the process slowly, very slowly.

You are standing in front of each other. Your ego starts the process which I have described above. On the basis of information from the emotional memory (a database), ego prepares to the process that will correspond with its idea. The boss will attack and it is necessary for you to defend yourself. It plays the movie to the mind. The body reacts to the mind with emotion. And now let us have a look at what is happening on the other side with the boss. His subconscious is also connected to the emotional memory (database), the same as you. But this time it's in a different (opposite) position, in the position (role) of the boss.

In the moment when your subconscious pulls out a card, where the boss is scolding his employee, the same card is mirroring in a signal which your subconscious is transmitting. The subconscious is not an instrument which sends over the signal, it is the signal itself. Metaphorically speaking, what is inside is mirroring the outside. The subconscious (what is inside) is mirroring on the outside. What is on the outside (the signal, frequency) perceives the subconscious of the boss and identifies with it. From an energy point of view, it is the most convenient thing to do (to align itself). It is playing the same card to its ego (to the ego of the boss), the same card, but its opposite side, the side of the boss. It is possible to say that this card contains the text of scenario of the further development. The bosses' ego is informed, as well as yours, about how the coming situation "should be" perceived, but only in the position of the boss. The card offers you the text: "The boss will curse and humiliate you." The boss will get his texts which are from the same card: "He ignores you. He doesn't stick together with you. He boycotts you on purpose, so that your boss will have to punish you."

Let's now play the action further. Both egos (yours and the bosses') will play this one card (movie) to their minds and the minds will play them to their bodies. Reactions will occur on both sides – emotions. The action is going on through a more or less obvious quarrel and conflict.

We will go even deeper and look at what preceded the situation before we came into the room where the boss and you (a carpenter) are standing opposite each other. You are working at your desk. Suddenly your colleague tells you, "You're supposed to go see the boss." He will add a particular tone of voice, an eye movement and body gesture to this statement, or he may not (but like this it is more obvious for our purposes). He is controlled by some present creature, it doesn't matter which one it is (maybe by the system of opposites which he of course does not realize at all, because he has been brought up in this system since childhood). The present creature, which controls him, wants to get energy and you and your boss were chosen for "milking". Just to clarify: this colleague is also under control by information from emotional memory – "a boss and an employee are in conflict all the time". Maybe your inner voice will speak out, especially if you have studied in the given field (human resources). It's a fact – persistent and potential conflict. The employee wants less work and more money. The boss wants more work for less money. It is coded (a curse) like that to the subconscious. It is a scenario created by present creatures which does not need to be fulfilled in every case.

The colleague who told you to go and see the boss had started it. This was the impulse, the frequency of emotional memory of the relationship between the employee and boss. "The boss will surely humiliate me" was the information chosen for ego.

On the other hand, the boss wants to know why something has not been done the way his boss wanted it to be done. Maybe he thinks he will consult with somebody or listen to the opinion of his employee who was supposed to take care of it. Maybe the boss is more interested in solving the problem than in punishing you.

You enter the room and before saying anything, a frequency that you send over (a signal from your subconscious), contacts a frequency of your boss. Immediately it will be clear which one was more conscious.

I will stop here. More conscious, in this context, means a state which we will be clarifying later. For better understanding I will now call it incorrectly, but in a way that you can understand. More conscious, in this context, means more supported by faith, conviction and certainty that this is exactly how it will end up.

If your frequency is more persuasive, the subconscious of your boss will accept to the game you offered. Here we are, back in (in the beginning of) the situation where you are standing opposite each other. The action will start to develop the way we have described above. In the moment when your ego is releasing its images (commentaries), his ego reacts. It is no longer about the fact that the boss wanted to know what happened. Emotions are spouting everywhere. The boss punishes and you suffer and maybe you are already putting together a plan of revenge. Present creatures are getting their share of energy out of these emotions.

So, once again. Absolutely independently on what happened in the moment (therefore there is an allergic reaction of the body with following emotion), the action turned out in a completely different way than it could have.

If you are standing in front of your boss and emanating a frequency, which I have described, the boss will react to it subconsciously. It does not mean that you were right because you had prepared for this properly and it still ended up in the same way. It is not like that. It ended this way exactly because you had prepared yourself for such an ending. Once again, we are touching on the theme of the creation of reality. You were emanating a certain frequency and to accept it was energetically the most convenient (but for whom – Existence, God?). Therefore, the other side (the boss) accepted it. Not consciously but unconsciously. It was energetically the most convenient because the boss is in a similar state of unconsciousness, as you are (otherwise he would "not have jumped on it"). If one of you were fully conscious, it would not have happened. He would have influenced the process along with his consciousness (his "signal" would have been "more conscious"). In that moment, it would be energetically more convenient to give in to his consciousness (which would have more "faith") than to use power to cancel out his power. Who works with this power, with consciousness? The answer is Existence, God. In the same way, you – if you were a conscious being – would influence the situation. This is where the transformation of consciousness leads to. Not letting yourself be controlled.

I will offer you another view of the whole situation. You have surely realized that the example I have used is a bit artificial but because of that is more understandable. It is important to grasp the principles of how this functions. The right examples will soon bring you your life (God). How could I know this? He brings them all the time. In fact, he will not start with it now, after you have finished reading this book. That's nonsense. He is here all the time, waiting with infinite patience for you to "open your eyes". The difference will now be in what you will already be able to realize, to see the signs which you have been constantly given.

Even deeper, under all this what we have described, is Fear. The more we deal with ourselves and connections, the deeper we go, the more often we will encounter this creature.

Fear in our artificial situation, is fear of our superiors. Maybe some do not realize that a boss also has his own boss. An employee is afraid of his boss. This boss is also afraid of his boss – a director perhaps. Everybody is afraid of his boss on an unconscious level. This fear has different forms. From very clear and concrete to more complicated ones, where a director is afraid of his boss who may be a little abstract, e.g. the shareholders of a company. In other cases, it could be the panel of a political party or voters. We could continue like this on and on.

One thing remains the same – fear. Where does this fear come from? It comes from childhood. It comes from the relationship between children and their parents. Parents were for example, the first bosses who you were afraid of.

Many powers and energies act in existence. As you become more conscious, the more of them you will be able to recognize and perceive. They will not be appearing because they have been here all the time, only you will gain the ability to perceive them. In fact, you will not even gain this ability, because you already have it. You will only realize this ability.

Some of these ancient principles have been used by ancient masters of martial arts (well known today) from the Far East. The statement: "my Wu-Shu is better than your Wu-Shu", or rather my martial art skills are better than yours, is a statement of ego. You can already perceive it yourselves, can't you? I am speaking about the period that preceded these times. When fighting was part of the art of survival and was not limited to fighting in the ring, according to the rules. At that time the physical fight was truly studied at different places of the planet as well, for example in the courts of kings. The masters of martial arts at that time were also masters of spiritual teachings. It isn't possible to separate physical fights and spiritual teachings, as some people wrongly believe. The teachers of martial arts were seeking both inner and outer harmony. They realized that with only one way they could not embrace the other one. Therefore, the most developed martial arts (often hidden from the public) also contained (applied) principles of spiritual teachings of certain places and periods. Grand masters of the arts showed mysterious moves and defeated their enemies in unusual ways. Many legends were born out of this. For us, it is important to realize (for the mind it is easier if we use examples) how such principles function. For this we will use an example from the physical fight.

One great teacher of the martial arts once said: "For each technique there is a contradictory technique, but you need time for it." The result was that the fighters tried to be faster than their rivals. They gradually discovered that the human body (its instincts) reacts faster than the body directed by the mind.

According to legends, ancient teachers observed animals and their natural movements. Natural movements of animals are devoid of thinking, so from a human point of view they are fascinating and above all, fast. Some of the fascinating styles of fight that were created are named after particular animals whose movements enchanted them. Above all, it is about instinctual movements. The teachers recognized that the mind stands in the way of the body's speed. That is why martial arts also contained different forms of meditation and spiritual exercises. During these activities they were trying to liberate the body from the dominance of the mind. To let the body react on the basis of its own intelligence.

Here is an example. If the body is preparing itself for a fight, then from a physiological point of view, certain physical changes take place (according to genetic information – DNA). Adrenalin widens the arteries, the blood pressure rises and so on. Real fighters know that if they are standing opposite each other and such processes are going on in their bodies, they have their last chance to start fighting. Otherwise, after a certain time their muscles will start shaking and they will lose their concentration. They know that speed comes out of absolute relaxation. What does absolute relaxation mean? Above all, it means relaxation of the mind, from thinking. I am sure you have seen someone who has touched a hot stove or saucepan by mistake. Maybe it has even happened to you. You pass by a hot stove and touch it with the back of your hand. A natural reaction of the body takes place. Your hand backs off as if it had been shot. Only in this phase, the mind enters the process and you (the own being) have been given information of what happened. But this is long after it happened. The body reacted as fast as was physically possible. It is not possible to physically react any faster. During that moment you hadn't even burned yourself. Our example is about the instinctive reaction of the body which is free from the mind's influence. The same with the fighter – the faster he wants to strike (begin the fight), the less he thinks about it. He concentrates and liberates his body from his mind (thinking). He imagines (creates reality) that he has already hit and struck first. In a masterful delivery it is a matter of split seconds when the above described processes go on in the mind. Similar principles are used for cracking various blocks of wood at exhibitions etc.

For us it is important to realize the fact that the body is able (more naturally) to react without the mind's control. It is necessary to fully realize this and give the body back its freedom. Faith in the body, that it is perfect and does not need any of the minds' interventions (for example various detoxifications, diets etc).

A similar example from the area of martial arts area is when it is energetically more convenient to step down (give in) to the pressure which your enemy is putting on you. Many martial arts use this principle and have developed it further. For example, they use their enemies' strength against the enemy himself. It is important to understand what "energetically more convenient" means.

This principle is widely applied in existence. If a big man rushes onto you and you are just a weak woman, then energetically it is more convenient not to oppose his pressure. Not to go towards him and clash with him. It is better to step aside and let the giant pass alongside. Try to grasp the principle of what is energetically more convenient. This principle is in existence, in the being. To keep this principle in existence – we can understand it also in the way that there are certain powers which "monitor" that big differences of potential will not arise. I will explain this immediately. If we have two different potentials, tension arises between them. Tension is not an energetically convenient state. "Energetically convenient" means that to maintain such a state, you need a smaller amount of energy than for the other. Tension is not an energetically convenient state because a huge amount of energy is consumed during it. Why? The reason is to keep a difference between particular potentials. The principle of existence works towards harmony of potentials and the disappearance of tension.

The most frequently used example is (of course) about fear. Imagine that you put two or three books on top of each other somewhere in the middle of a room. You stand on this pile of books in such a way that the tips of your shoes overlap towards the front. You are actually standing only on a part of your feet and a part is in the air, a few centimeters above the floor. You are only standing, maybe rocking slightly, back and forth. You do not sense anything extraordinary. Now, imagine that you do the same on the edge of the roof of a tall building. Suddenly, some emotions come. Mistrust in yourself, in the material of the roof's edge and so on. Fear is here. More sensitive people might even have the feeling that something is pushing them off the edge. Either off the roof or a few steps back from the edge. They cannot even bear thinking of that kind of situation. Nobody likes being in that kind of position. For some people just the thought of standing a few meters in front of the edge paralyzes them so much that they cannot go any further.

We are now speaking about other creatures (powers) inhabiting this reality. In the above mentioned example the principle of energy convenience intervenes. In the moment when the human being (a person) starts to produce emotions of fear, the potential in intangible reality immediately starts to be produced. This does not correspond with the reality (presence) in the tangible (material) reality. This is the difference between potentials. Simply said, there is a movie showed to the mind about you falling off the roof. But of course, this is not true.

The reality is that you are standing on the edge. If you put a brick at the same place, nothing happens, the same applies if you put it in the middle of a room. All of this can happen only if someone supplies the process with energy. That someone is a human being. Energy, produced through the unity of the mind and the own being, is the power almost equal to the ability to influence reality. In such a moment, you are in a very similar state, as if you are influencing reality, the tangible world. You create such a huge potential that surrounding existence will interfere. How? In such a way that it will put the whole situation into an energetically more convenient state. It will either pull you down (this is what you feel) or it will pull you back. The process on the edge is not sustainable from a long-term point of view.

If you are very scared of something, then you can be sure that your worries will come true. You have to either dissolve your worries, or they will become real. What you experience inside will appear on the outside – you will influence the reality surrounding you, along with what you experience inside. On top of that, if emotion arises, a certain kind of "free" energy comes into being as well. Because energy is a valuable currency, it will not stay unused for long. Other present creatures will start coming to such a place. If Ego succeeds in occupying "one of the first positions", an addiction to so called adrenalin sports may arise.

Adrenalin Sports

Adrenalin sports are activities where people purposely get into situations similar to our example with the roof's edge. It does not need to be only with sports, it's similar with some motorcyclists too. A person will bring himself to a state where he is very close to death (sometimes a very brutal death). He tries to experience this state, so that he evokes emotion for himself on purpose. We know what emotions do to the physical body. These emotions feed Ego, more often not only Ego, especially if the person is a part of an organized activity. His body suffers but the movie screened to the darkened mind is fascinating, so the body continues its activity. But in this case it is a bit different. The body itself, in fact, its memory (DNA), also takes part. The body agrees to the activity at a certain level. Therefore, the body is not quickly destructed, whereas the body of the mentally ill is (you can see the most obvious changes with the obsessed).

The bodies of people which do adrenalin sports are in much better shape, especially if the sport contains some kind of physical endurance. What is the difference? In similar states, a certain kind of fear that is not mutated is kept in the body's genetic memory from the times (from the place of existence) where the fight for life, e.g. with animals, was taking place. A certain kind of will (agreement) to realize (experience) such situations remained in the body. It is the body's reaction (adrenalin) to an anticipated and defined feeling, a state of a physical attack, a battle. This is not emotion because it is a real state. The body analyses the coming information through its intelligence. This is similar to adrenalin sports but with the difference in that they are not really endangering because these activities are controlled by present creatures. The body, at the level of genetic memory, agrees with the existing state and this is why the poison, which arises during emotion, becomes partly neutralized, but only to a certain extent, which is different with every person according to the genetic memory of his or her body. If a limit is exceeded, the person dies. It ends up being called an unlucky coincidence. That is a mistake. Only the limit that the body could "bear" or permit, was exceeded. Then emotion had the same course as we have described before. And considering that the body (probably) had acted as a catalyst for a long time, emotion grew into a huge power. As soon as the body stopped influencing the process, this power was released and in tangible reality killed the physical body in a single moment. This is apparent especially during sports and activities where energy, created in such a way, is not immediately transmitted by the physical body for example to muscle activity. Then the arising poison is less "diluted" and the end comes "absolutely unexpectedly".

If you look at the development of adrenalin sports from the view of how they are distributed on the planet, you will see an interesting thing. Adrenalin sports are much more frequent in "quieter" countries where the inhabitants (especially men) are not in very close contact with death. Sports like parachute jumping from a skyscraper, climbing a building without protective ropes, free-fall jumps, mountain bike free riding or skiing in areas with a risk of avalanches, fast riding on a motorbike, you will probably not find much in countries like Afghanistan, Iraq and similar. In these places, the needs of present creatures are satisfied more naturally (according to both historical and current situations).

There is no simple answer to the question why people want to do these sports. That is why I am using these examples to show how wide the issue of present creatures is. So that we can realize what is connected with what and were able perceive connections. I am sure that you will find many answers to this question yourself. The easiest answer is that Ego controls these sport enthusiasts. This is without a doubt the right answer. Another influence is the coded will to risk in our DNA which can, without any control, make us want to take risks. We could continue like this on and on.

The reason, why I have used this example, is different. It is a mystery that you can read "between the lines". We could state many other reasons and all of them would be more or less correct. We could focus on many things but the one that really matters would have escaped us.

It is the feeling that you control reality. As I said, the feeling you have during these sports is very similar (not the same!) to the one which you experience when you influence the reality around you. This is the main reason which is shrouded by all the others. It is a natural (inborn) need.

We will explain one word here – inborn. An inborn need is one you have had naturally since birth, since you were born. It is in-born (birth). It is given to us as a part of our "equipment".

Yes, I'm talking about your ability to change, create reality, to create all that surrounds you – the world, space. Human beings have an inborn = innate ability to create and to influence. This ability has been and still is hidden from you by gods and present creatures. We all have this ability, nobody is particularly elected.

But this feeling is a bit misleading. It confuses feelings and real free will which is expressed during creation, with emotions experienced not only during such sports. Sports, in general, work with emotions and especially with ego. We are talking about organized sports. But private sport falls also into this category if it is motivated by volition. **Volition is an expression of ego.**

Organized sportsmen want to win for themselves, for their clubs and for their salaries.

A girl, who runs every day, wants to lose weight. She has the feeling that she is not beautiful enough the way she is. Maybe she even feels beautiful apart from the fact that she has to lose a little weight, at least on her thighs. Why does she feel like this if the men around her are happy with her body? Maybe they would be even happier if she were a little curvier. Why doesn't she see herself through their (much more objective) eyes? An analogy with anorexia would be fitting here. Men do not like bony women. I'll give another example. A young man who goes to the gym regularly wants to have (bigger) muscles. He destroys his body by hours of exercise and by various chemical supplements. Although women do not particularly like such types of men.

Why are all these people doing such absurd things? All people want something. They are controlled by Ego (via their ego). Where does this come from? Why is it like that?

We can already understand how a person controlled by a present creature acts. We are now trying to understand the trigger point of potential loss of being in charge of yourself.

Loss of Freedom

We will analyze the question of the girl who does sports. Here is a clarification graspable for the mind.

A person has the feeling that they must lose weight

A person has the feeling that they must lose weight; a person, a human being. We spoke about how to perceive human beings, what creates them and what they contain. You have found out that human beings are Trinitarian beings influenced by their seven energy centres located in the human body. These centers – chakras have certain qualities and abilities. They can be functional, only partly functional or not functional at all.

A person **has** the feeling that they must lose weight, so he owns – has something. Something becomes a part of himself. Something is inside him, something is himself. He **has** a feeling.

A person has **the feeling** that they must lose weight – with this example, notice and realize "where is the problem". The feeling is a certain frequency, information – energy which is created in human beings. The state before – you feel something – comes to the human body from the front, from the outside. It enters the body. There is something happening inside the body. These feelings modulate energy-information flows between single substances of a trinitarian human being. Simply said, the substances "communicate" with each other; the physical body, the own being (soul) and the spirit. Everything is still fine but only if the feeling can leave the body in the form of free will. Then it would **leave** through the back channel of an energy field, **chakra, which is continuous**. But this would mean that we could not say that we have a feeling because we would **not have** it, we would only perceive it. We would only perceive – feel it coming through us, modulating and influencing other parts of our being. We would perceive other processes, communication, reactions and the like. Of course this did not happen (in the example). What happened was that **a person had a feeling**. Whatever you say is being realized (created). A person having a feeling means that the feeling remained in themselves (in the person). It did not go through the energy system (chakras) in the form of free will. **The feeling remained in the physical body and became an emotion.** Yes, we can see another example of how emotion arises. That is why emotions and feelings are often confused and most people are not able to diffe-rentiate between them.

Feelings are a natural part of embodiment. You **have** a feeling after the feeling went through your body and was affected by your mind. Feelings (pure feelings) have been affected by your mind and afterwards you **have** a feeling. "To have a feeling" is a state which comes after the contact between a feeling and a human being, in fact with the mind. Therefore, it is not true that you will become an unfeeling person by transforming your con-sciousness; not at all. You will not even be without fee-lings and emotions. In fact they will not disappear from your life. They will appear time to time but will no longer control you.

You will not only know what it is all about, but above all, you will be able to influence it. To influence it in the way that is convenient for you. I am sure you know from your own experience, moments when you needed to have a calm voice but it was shaking or skipping occasionally. You may act in (for you) an emotionally intense situa-tion and fall over your own feet. Here is an example for all. A woman knows she needs to leave her husband. She will do everything so that she can do so. Suddenly, the man appears and she, influenced by emotions from seeing him, doesn't leave. Was this free will? This is doubtful. It is obvious that this influence has been used (abused) not only by present creatures but also by other people for a very long time.

Back to decoding. A person has the feeling they have to lose weight. We already understand the first part of this statement. Now we will look at the second part. Someone has the feeling that they **must** lose weight – because they must, it is a duty. **Duty comes out of the absence of free will**. If you have free will, you are free, and then you really don't have to. You will just go and do it. You simply do it because you need to. This has a completely different vibration. That you have to do something is a **symptom of duty, it is pressure**. Pressure causes counter-pressure, this is what you feel if you are fulfilling any kind of duty. If you are free (conscious) enough to feel. Again, you can sense it as a difference between potentials, which is an energetically inconvenient process which will be sooner or later eliminated by intervention from "the above". It means that if duty has a symptom of pressure, it is not natural for you and you will soon abandon it because it will not be effective for you.

It won't have the effect you need. If I generalize even more, you simply will not be happy. So, if you dutifully go running and you don't eat much, you will probably lose weight after a while. But you will not look the way you imagined. You will lose weight on other parts of your body than the ones you wanted. You may even get health problems and so on.

A person has the feeling they must **lose weight** – to change themselves. Here is another mistake. You cannot change yourself. Perfection is in oneness and entireness. You are naturally whole. This means that you are perfect. So, the change can only cause imperfection. It will let loose further searching and activities leading back to perfection, to the original state. This will go round and round in vicious circles. Your intention is not to change yourself, but to be yourself. If this happens – then many things in your life will change, especially perception. How you perceive (and how you realize) and also how you are perceived by your surroundings. Then you will also physically look the way you would like. If you are balanced inside, you will be balanced on the outside (body, skin, hair, nails etc.).

A person has the feeling they must **lose weight**. In this you can see that **the true intention is to lose weight**. Surely you know questions like: "What weight does your decision have?" – "What weight does your word carry?" In our example, the person is changing, losing weight. It is clear that **to change yourself means to lose weight, to become someone else**, but only on the surface, because it is not possible on the inside. Absolute devotion and obstinacy will change you physically (always with health effects) but deep down inside it will still be you. Still unhappy and unsatisfied.

The statement we used is a big illusion. You may think that whatever you say is used against you. It can be true under certain circumstances. The word creates and to use it unconsciously can be a source of many problems. Does it mean that it is better not to speak at all? Truly said, it is a certain phase of development. But it is not a duty. If you look at all the prophets (in other words, conscious beings, people), each of them went through a silent period. It is often connected with other esoteric sensations. Of course, many modern mystics are also aware of the power of silence as a key to (heavenly) gates, which silence opens to those who listen. To become silent is a very convenient tool for independent discovery. Humility as a big enemy of ego is related to this.

If we enlighten the preceding statement, it is clear that it leads down a blind alley. Then where did the even deeper loss of freedom originate?

It is that everybody feels imperfect, incomplete and not integrated. We are getting closer to an essential discovery! Why do people feel like that? It is again about ego, but this time in an unexpected position.

Ego is Afraid

As we have shown before on previous pages, we can also analyze the sentence: **Ego is afraid**.

Ego – we know who (what) it is. In fact we have been recognizing it and discovering it all the time. It is a present creature, an energy-information entity which has a direct connection to one substance (soul) of the human being.

Is – fear is a part of it. Fear, in this sense, is a part of Ego.

Afraid – fear as a feeling, is connected with death at the lowest (tangible) level. You are afraid (your ego is afraid) of not being accepted as you are, of death, in a certain sense. Either physical death or for example career death (they will reject you as a model or an expert), lovers (your partner rejects you for your imperfection, because you will not respond to what he wants), family (your family will reject you, your father, mother, because you have not fulfilled their expectations of your education or life path). **Ego reacts on the basis of fear**. It means that the origin is ego's feeling. **The essential substance of fear is separation.** At this place, Death arose. This has been said in many texts. Yet not understood by many. Human beings are perfect (divine) and as such are immortal and mortality is given by fear (again, we can see the antithesis light – dark, life – death).

Let us shed light on the frequent theme of devil, a negative power, a frequency of fear which for many is represented by the term Lucifer.

Fear (the same as the mind) is often ascribed to this entity. Lucifer, which means "a torchbearer", was thrown from heaven (light) into the dark (shadows) to reign in hell, in darkness. Current Christian spiritual teachings talk about him as of a fallen angel (originally a messenger of god). Here, we can find the original non-acceptance and from this arose original fear. Lucifer was rejected (not accepted) by god. Again, the same applies, **"you cannot give what you do not have yourself"**.

How should we understand this? The god, who rejected Lucifer, could not have been "the original" first God, Creator, Existence. **God is unconditional acceptance. God is endless love.** God (Existence) accepts unconditionally, in fact he accepts himself, he is everything. Only the absence, the lack of unconditional acceptance could have led to the rejection of the torchbearer into the shadows. Fear has transformed itself into an independent creature, through ways that are not yet understood and has shadowed much. It puts mass into the way of light (God) and like this it throws shadows (the absence of light) on the Earth (Mother). This is where the original fear comes from. That is why it is also possible that you are not satisfied, or are even disgusted by a part of your body. God did the same with his torchbearer, in fact with a part of himself. Here lies the original sin. Not the sin of man but of a god. This is what Lucifer wanted men to understand; to recognize that the true god is something else. Do not confuse this with Satanism or other similar systems.

We will go back to the cross. We have said that the cross means an intersection of space and time. Now I am offering you another explanation. The vertical part is space, god. The horizontal part is time, Lucifer. If water falls down, it symbolizes the flow of God's power. Water falls onto a vertical obstacle (mass – mind) and splashes drops. Lucifer is a vertical obstacle. At the place where water splashes into drops and "water dust" and together with the presence of light (spirit), **rainbow – a symbol of a human** appears. Rainbow colors correspond to the particular energy fields of the human body.

Light is the finest form of mass, light itself does not throw shadows. If mass steps into the way of light, a shadow will appear. But in the presence of light, shadows disappear again. For this it is necessary to change the point of view (of the light's shine). So, as mass (the mind) steps into the way of light (truth) all the time, it is necessary to keep changing the angle of shine all the time. This is a movement which is an accompanying phenomenon of all life.

Separation is an essential substance of fear, therefore, disunity, a lack of entirety and incompleteness. It is necessary to grasp these words. Fear is the one that tells you (through the mouth of your ego or mind) that you are imperfect. In fact, it is afraid that it will (again) be rejected. It is not you who is afraid! Only mortals are afraid. Mortality is a broad-spectrum concept. It is a complex theme. Complex = made up of multiple parts and layers. Everything what the transformation of consciousness deals with is complex. It is made up, at the same time, of many simple parts and places.

We will clarify the (im)mortality of Ego. As we have said, the ego has many layers. It acts for itself as the ego belonging to a particular human being – as a part of a human being. At the same time, Ego exists in higher forms. In forms which are, in their own way, superior to individual egos. There are more of these levels. Its mortality and also certain immortality lies in the fact that the ego as an intangible entity dies with the physical body (it is its part) but at the same time does not die as it is an intangible entity. The ego, at its low level, is not aware of this fact. Instead it perceives itself as mortal because it is connected with the physical body which contains death in a part of its genetic information. So, it knows about it (about death). At high levels, Egos do not perceive mortality as a primary problem. They are aware (and this is the main problem = Egos are already aware) that mortality is not related to them directly. In other words, as long as the last enslaved man with a controlled ego lives, a higher Ego will also exist. Egos rather perceive a form of their existence, that they are essentially not embodied, as a problem.

At a basic level ego is mortal. This is information which Fear gives to your ego. Fear works with presence, with powerful force and is, thanks to presence, trustworthy. Lucifer's experience of rejection is present in Fear's genetics. It gives this frequency (similar to emotional memory) to ego which influences the mind on the basis of this frequency. The mind creates a hypothesis that this will happen (for sure) again and starts other processes in the body. The whole chain of processes is, simply said, started by ego's fear of death (the end), of rejection. This fear is so strong (present) that it influences all further processes and development of human being's existence.

If you need to understand the principle that starts the feeling of imperfection, realize that it is a feeling which you have inside you. It is a captured feeling in the body which did not go through you further as free will (from tangible to intangible). The same as Fear, as an intangible creature, it was captured "in the body" (in this reality) as a feeling – fear – and it was not let go of as a manifestation of free will. The other way around, it has been captured in many systems and everything negative is subscribed to fear.

This concrete feeling was the lack of love (demonstrated by rejection) which remained present as a feeling – fear of rejection. It remained present – this means that it uses the power of presence. It is present. Feeling – the lack of love (there was not unconditional acceptance) is realized (imprisoned, it cannot go through, leave) as the feeling of fear of rejection. This is genetic information that people have inside themselves. Because of the god that punishes (without love), that god which rejected his angel (Lucifer). Was this a big mistake or an intention...?

In many texts (translated currently) and especially in the Bible, God is confused with a god and gods. This is a total misunderstanding or an intentional confusion of the truth. These are difficult issues. Here, it is necessary to at least realize where your perfection, you divine origin has been influenced. It was at the place where **conditional acceptance** arose. Influenced by some gods, creatures with the highest consciousness at the given place of reality. Many of them were originally humans. Legends and myths clearly give such evidence. Many words and names bear witness to this, for example, the word Israel, translated loosely, means "fighting with god" (notice the present tense). You must be starting to perceive the connections in an extra sensory way and this is only the beginning.

If conditional acceptance arose, it created the substance of fear. It unwinds from here. Now you know where fear comes from. **Fear comes from conditional acceptance.** It is about acceptance, conditional love, love only with conditions. An example: "I will love you but only if you are faithful to me." This statement contains many issues which need to be clarified. Now, let's explain what conditional acceptance is. This kind of acceptance invokes fear. "What if he thinks that I'm not faithful?" Whether you are faithful or not, is not possible to prove. Women can probably understand me now more than men. One of the problems of this statement is a twisted definition and combining of various frequencies regarding love, being in love, love making, sex, acceptance and the like. As I said, this statement is much wider, but you can realize what conditional acceptance is. Be aware of that it brings fear into your presence. Fear of non-acceptance, which in this statement, stands on both sides. On the side of the man who is speaking because he feels threatened, uncertain (with himself mostly) that he will be abandoned – rejected (thrown down into the shadows), not accepted by the woman. On the side of the woman – she has been chained down because she is not accepted either – by the man, unconditionally. So, she is not free and a poison of doubts is injected into her being. Both of them are unhappy, both of them suffer because of this statement, in fact by the fear contained in the statement.

Fear comes from non-acceptance, from rejection. That is why ego is scared. Here is the origin of the absence of freedom, feelings of incompleteness (disintegrity) and disunity. For better comprehension, we will explain these expressions. The lack of freedom is clear.

It is the central theme which the transformation of consciousness deals with. Disintegrity is a loss of integrity, so you are missing something. You are missing unconditional acceptance. Disunity is a loss of unity. With the trinitarian – human – being, it means disharmony of its particular substances. Disharmony between the own being, which knows that it is immortal, and the physical body, that carries information about death in its memory. The mind, under the pressure of the body's information and ego's feelings cannot then do anything else but to accept it. Disharmony of the soul and the mind occurs, in other words, disharmony of the substance of the physical body and the substance of the own being. The mind as the being, on the border of intangible and tangible realities, which had put itself into the position of the body's spokesman, cannot find a common language with the own being. The mind often in its blindness does not see what it is doing. As we said, it is most of all because the mind (tangibly) is above eye level.

The Step to Freedom

The more we plunge into relations created in existence which influence our reality, the more you will be gaining a true picture. You already understand that it is not possible to ignore religion because it has significantly affected the lives of people on this planet. You already understand that it is necessary to recognize, understand, realize and accept the existence of everything as it is. You realize that the wheel of your decision making is controlled by various helmsmen and it is necessary to fully take over the chance to be in charge of your being, your existence. It is not possible to adopt a way of thinking: "us and them" (again opposites), the way which is typical rather for unchained Ego than for a conscious human being. It is necessary to recognize different relations and to realize them, to understand why some things happen. To grasp and accept, forgive mistakes to those who do not know what they are doing. To give up your own importance and to find humility. To be yourself. It is necessary to recognize the games that have been played, are being played and are being prepared to be played. In this reality, it is possible to realize much more than the mind and science show. Set yourself free of dogmas and start to fly if you need to. Walk on water. Travel through time. This all is possible, right here. Stop spending your life with activities that turn you away from knowing the truth. Set yourself free! Liberate yourself!

We began with the example of the conflict with the boss. We described how emotion is created. Now you know that one of the ways present creatures can control you is through emotion. Let's get back to this. I will describe a technique of what to do.

If you realize the above stated information, we can start with the technique itself.

It can be good for you to go back to the pages where we deal with emotions – how they come about and what they do (control).

In the moment when you perceive that control is coming or if you are already in the first phase of control, realize that light does not fight. **Light simply is**. Use this principle, this magic. Do not fight with anything or anybody, not even with yourself. A fight is a fight and the result is, once again, fight. **"Just" be**.

If you say that you are struggling with something, either out loud or internally, you identify yourself with it and you are condemning yourself to failure. This is hell on earth. You are using the power of the presence, but against yourself. How? If you say for example: "I am struggling with smoking, I want to quit", or you say "I am thinking of how to do it, I am dealing with it all the time." Then, you have pronounced a curse of failure. You are using (present time) to describe the process. This means that you give the power of presence to the process. You give it the ability to realize itself, to in-fluence reality. If you say that you are fighting with something – this is it – fighting. Then what result can this statement have? That you win? Or that you lose? Neither of them! The effect of fighting in presence is only fighting. Neither victory nor failure. Only fighting. This is hell. When you deal with something without really solving it! You curse the process (reality) by the power of word multiplied by the power of presence to an endless loop, a cycle – that "it is happening", without requiring the process to finish, to end. It is because the statement ends in the present. Sure, with the promise of the future, but the future does not exist yet. Only the presence exists and if you lock the process in pre-sence by the curse, it is not possible to change it. This is a vicious circle. Do you understand? I will repeat it once again, it is necessary that you realize it. The statement "I am fighting with it", is the statement of the process which is locked in the time (present) loop. The result is nothing more than endless "fighting".

The first step is to **realize yourself**. Say yourself in spirit: "I am". Ego says words like: "me, my, mine". In this moment, you are defining yourself in space, in reality, in existence. This is really necessary. It defines you – it gives you the space for being and for the realization of yourself. In the words "I am", you realize yourself in existence, in present reality. This is very important. If you say these words, you say everything that is needed and all who you really are gets activated. It is not a job position, an accomplished education or anything like that. We are talking about you, your own being, about who you really are. Who you are from the own being's point of view, not from the ego's view (under the reign of the male principle). The description would be as wide as the awareness of the one who is describing it. It depends on how many connections they would be able to realize. This is all contained in the words "I am". It does not create some new space but it makes obvious the fact that you are here. Your space which you already have is influenced by you, in the way that you inhabit the space. You are in unity, integrity and entirety. You are yourself. There is no place for uninvited guests. Without any fight.

As the second step, realize the presence. **Be present by your whole being.** Immediately, you will feel a flow of energy. Nobody is helping you, you can forget that. It is you yourself who controls this. Such power you have if you are present. If you say and realize in spirit: **I am present**, you will gain huge power. The power of the word is endless. If you say something in spirit, it means that you accept the cooperation of the spirit in the sense of God. This way is much more powerful, it is realized instinctively as soon as you manage this technique. You are present, some space has been created between you and anything what emotion (its information element) brings. In this moment, you are isolated from the information element of emotion. This is a very important step. The information element is for example, in the statement: "He is making fun of you!" You are present and you know what and who is now active. You know that the only reason why this all is happening is to deprive you of your energy. Do not allow it. It will not be easy in the beginning. It is enough for you to take small steps forward. First realize that it is happening and what is in fact happening. Use the principles of light (non-fighting) and the principle of the presence (freedom).

We said that the presence is a very short moment, as short as you can make it. This moment is separated from another present moment by a crossroad (the cross) of decision making. Then, the next present moment comes and like this it goes on and on.

If **you are** present you can take advantage of other divine principles. Now, we will discover another divine power. You already know the power of the word. Now, we will talk about the power of silence, because: **silence is golden**. What does that mean? It means a certain state of mind – an unconscious mind. If you speak – you create, the word creates. Not only the word itself, but also the sound that accompanies the word when you pronounce it. The sound is also a certain frequency. You know that the word has the power to create if spoken both out loud or internally – in spirit (realize this statement –

"pronounced in spirit"). If the mind is unconscious (influenced), then it can (and it of course does) pronounce things not convenient for you, in fact the opposite. The statement "silence is golden" comes from this. If you do not pronounce (neither aloud nor in spirit), you are not tossed about by your thoughts, then you are silent. The color gold is connected with the seventh chakra, a very specific one. It symbolizes the spirit and consciousness but also love and infinity. If you are silent on the inside and the outside, then you dwell in silence. Silence can talk to you at the direct level of consciousness. If you are silent, you begin to perceive what you do not hear. Silence speaks. You perceive what is perceivable (realizable) only in the space of freedom. Free = unconditional, uncontrolled. In this moment you are receiving the information from the Core, from the Source, from God. It is also because you are present. With this we get back to presence itself and this clarification precedes the question that is coming.

How to Be Present?

We can use various methods. Some religious directions have worked with pain. But this is not functional, pain is connected with the body (mass, space) and also with time, but the presence is out of time.

We can use one of the four basic elements – air. There are many techniques and especially Eastern teachings attach weight to these. You can understand air also as breath. Breathing is a basic element of most meditation techniques. Why is this?

Ancient masters of these arts were aware of the power of the presence. At the same time, they were aware of how difficult it is for the beginner, to free himself from continuous thinking. Thinking over and over is in fact a continuous process, a struggle which concerns the future or the past. It is not compatible with the presence. They were using breathing as a method of staying present. If you work consciously with your breath, you will immediately become present, as if by miracle. More precisely said, you will not leave the presence. This technique is frequently used and other (Western) systems of this planet have also been working with it.

How to use breath for finding the presence? Start at home in simple conditions. Sit down and close your eyes. Now, observe your breath. Observe both inhalation and exhalation. Focus on the inside, not on the outside manifestation of your breathing, like sound and body movement. Sense the air coming in and coming out. It is not necessary to imagine anything, colors, shapes, directions etc. In the moment when you are dealing with the breath itself, the state of presence will come. Your mind is free of the past and of the future. Free from all thoughts. As soon as you realize this, doubts, thoughts and voices will come. It does not matter, you have already experienced the state very close to the presence, you know that it is possible and how it feels.

There are many techniques of working with breath and meditation. Many books have been written about it, so we will not be dealing here with this technique for long. Do not try to find in this technique more than what it is (by repeating the mistake of many "spiritual teachers"). As we said, everything is equally important. The question of importance is false. Use the principles we have been reminding or uncovering for your own needs. Do not let yourself be controlled. Accept what is necessary for you and go on. The path to creation of reality leads through the recognition of yourself, because what is inside creates what is outside. We are now in time, more exactly said at the place of existence where it is possible to influence from the inside. It is a manifestation of the female principle.

I will remind you for a moment of the relations between the male and the female principles. These two principles have come into existence at places which are not precisely identifiable (from the current point of view). Tangible and intangible existence was differently connected than it is now. Conscious beings (predecessors of people) which had then existed were asexual and impregnation happened intangibly through an organ placed in the head, by the activity of certain frequencies from the outside. This organ was at the same time both a sensory and communication instrument of these beings. We are speaking about times when the Earth was connected with other universal orbs (the way we perceive them today), about the times when the opposites were not yet defined.

Gradually, as reality has been changing, planets had arisen and the Earth had separated. Separation started to arise. Here we can find clarification of relations of upper and bottom chakras, as the symbol of the Jewish candlestick shows (see the third part of the book – The Mystery of Creation). Until then it was not possible to perceive and realize the way as we know it today. The beings were connected with the Existence (God) that much they were not aware of themselves really.

Here you can see a certain allegory with Adam and Eve and their relation to sex. The more the tangible forms were observed and realized, the more separation of sexuality, to male and female sexuality, was taking place. This was the expulsion from the Paradise. Adam and Eve had realized it and could not stay any longer. Here we can also realize the creation of the male and the female principle. Everything was different. By birth and development of senses, the spiritual substance in the human being has been divided. A part of the substance to the body and a part to the own being. In that from what the human brain has developed, the way we know the brain today, some centres of the brain were losing its importance. The mind – the front brain had come to the forefront because the more it has been used (sensory perception) the more it has grown physically. Then it pushed at other parts of the brain in the head and they were escaping (e.g. the hind-brain). Human beings had been materializing. The male outer principle was recognizing reality and entering the outside life. The female inner principle was withdrawing. Here we can also find the Mother (the Earth) and the Father (God) as the Sun. Creation of energy fields on human body and other. As senses have been developing, also the breath was influenced. The breath that was not directly attached just to life as it is today, had also the inner (female – original) part. Thanks to this primeval aspect of the breath we can use it now.

Jesus knew this and this was called the Holy Grail (female principle). The female primary principle with its magic abilities. In the times of Egypt, the female power was perceived and honored as a healing power. In the opposite were the methods of inquisition against women in the medieval times.

*Back to our theme, the above text is the less understandable, the less the mind controls your own being. The transformation of consciousness is recognition of yourself and of the world surrounding you. Senses (male method) are not enough for that, it is necessary to perceive in an extra sensory way (female manner). This is the real mystery of the Holy Grail.

We were seeking presence in observation of breath. Try this technique at a still place where nothing disturbs or annoys you.

We have shown two steps of how to react if you were attacked by a present creature. To realize what is happening (outer) and realize self (inner). Not let yourself be influenced by what ego or the mind say. Be in silence of these voices. If necessary, remind yourself that you are by stating: "I am". Not to fight (disagree) because through fighting (disagreement) you would energetically take a part in the whole situation without achieving anything.

It is also necessary to breath enough. Use the presence connected with breath, it is necessary to breath the whole body through.

Now, we are getting to other connections of the work with emotions. We have already said that emotion is a poison which goes through the body. To enable the body to get rid of the poison, it is necessary to breath. It is a natural reaction of the body. At any difficult situation, the body always instinctively increases the frequency of breathing. It can be difficult to perceive this need in the beginning. So, do not rely on body instincts but try to breath consciously whenever you meet emotions. Use it for grounding, strengthening yourself in the presence for example. You will consciously involve the element of air (breath) for your own benefit. At the same time, involve the element of water. Water transfers information. It is an intangible interaction. The less pure water you drink, the more you body is weakened because of the lack of information. You are working with information, now. Drink enough of pure water, the human body is created of water most of all. Listen to the needs of your body, it will let you know what it really needs. The human body is as important as the human soul is. This body is affected by the four elements of this reality.

If you find the aspects of the female principle, which will strengthen you in searching for presence, in air and water, then seek them also in remaining elements. The aspects are hidden there. Fire as another element represents warmth. Keep your body comfortable in warmth, take care of it. Cold is accompanied with feelings of fear and the other way around. The last one is the element of earth, the mass. It is connected with touch, with realizing and experiencing the touch. Touch yourself, discover, sense and love your body, all its parts. To love – the ancient meaning of this word is to realize. If you do not express love and a feeling of belonging to your body, then the body cannot be a real support to you. You can give only what you have. The same with the body, it can give only what it has. The element of earth represents also the Earth as the Mother, so learn from the Earth. Observe it how it is present.

How present are the material forms. Observe flowers, trees, stones.

If you allow it, you can benefit of all the four elements when searching for and finding the presence.

The Sign of the Cross, the Presence

Once again, we will stop here and uncover another mystery. At the time of Jesus' crucifixion, another two men were crucified. One of them was talking to Jesus and asked him for forgiving. The faith of men was differently strong in different times. The state we have been aiming by harmony of the mind and soul, was much more natural in other times. Harmony of the mind and soul was more natural because the mind had not dominated as much. People did not understand to many things but they were more humble. This can bring fear but also deeper faith. Thanks to it, people were able to perceive and realize faster in certain situations. This was the case of the crucified man who had experienced a state of entire consciousness before he died. By the power of the word and the power of the presence, Jesus relieved this man of pain. How? He had brought him through his faith to the state of entire consciousness. Just through his faith, the man sentenced to death reached this state. If you are present, you are out of time, out of the past and out of the future, you are now. In presence, the crucified did not feel pain when dying. He was out of time and space, he already stood out of the System (using words of the Bible – he was in Paradise).

Through the presence atonement and liberation is possible. Of what? Of control. How are you controlled? By emotions. Emotion is a tool for controlling but it is not necessary to fight with it. It is necessary to accept it. To accept means to give up. To accept does not mean to tolerate anything, anyone's behavior. **To accept means to give up in the sense of giving up the own importance.** In front of whom and of what? In front of yourself, only surrender in front of yourself has a real meaning. To give up your own importance. To give up everything. If you give up everything, then you are not attached to anything. You are free. If you are not attached, then you are not vulnerable. Beware of the words. The statement: "You are not vulnerable." is not same as: "You are invulnerable".

This is a very important wisdom. It has been used by people in different fields. Let's say, used by the more conscious people. What does it mean? By people who reached a higher level of consciousness. Most of all, not because they would want it but because they needed it.

The enlightened people appear in the worst conditions from the human's (mind's) judgment. Very often they come from the worst conditions, broken families, material discomfort and so on. There are also exceptions, e.g. Siddhartha Gautama (Buddha) who was born and had lived in material wealth, but later he left voluntarily, he gave up everything. Is it then necessary to be either poor or sick to reach enlightenment? No, it is not necessary in this time. But the truth is that people very often start to think differently only after experiencing a difficult life situation or at the edge of life. For example, after a bad accident a man will realize in the hospital what passing values he preferred. But very often, these glimpses of awareness disappear quickly after recovery and are replaced by sensations of a present creature that keeps a man artificially in mourning or self-pity (of his fate).

* Note : Hands going "numb"
   ↳ energy being absorbed by
     environment!! (theory)

The example of surrender we find at warriors who were giving up their lives not because they would misprize it (the real warrior does not do it, it is the position of Ego). They only did not put such importance on life, and this untied their hands (martial arts) and also the mind (strategy). We can also say that they were giving up ownership of life, power over life and they put their lives into the power of various gods, teachings and so on. These warriors had found their faith this way. Therefore, they were winning, were less afraid and had more faith than their enemies.

You can find a similar example in today prisons. Every prisoner knows (recognizes very quickly) that if he cares about something, it is his weak point. In prison, anyone can abuse this to captivate him. Very quickly you learn not to fix to anything what you can lose.

By giving up of your relationship to something or someone, you become free to it/him. You give your freedom also to your counterpart (a thing, a person). You give what you really have. This liberation is very important in the relationship with your own children.

Therefore, those who live the "difficult" life full of problems reach enlightenment earlier. Do you think that those who you consider to be happy are really happy and free? That it cannot happen to you? Do you think that you are too sinful, ignorant and unconscious? That you do not have any extra sensory skills, you do not see aura or you do not even believe in God? Nonsense. God is calling by the strongest voice the strayest sheep. The ones who are the most distanced to themselves.

In other words, the ones of you who do not feel any extraordinary skills yet, will be the most surprised. The ones who, until now, have governed themselves with their minds. Their faith will be the most solid because it will spring from the need to be, not from the pressure – to want more! In addition to that, such strong mind will be also a strong "cooperate" in faith. I mean now absolutely concrete faith – the faith in yourself! No proof will persuade you more than your own. So, the proof for your mind, experienced by yourself in the presence. Therefore, do not try to persuade anyone else by your proofs and experience. Who did not experience it himself, will not believe.

TRUTH!!

Now Thomas (called Didymus), one of the Twelve, was not with the disciples when Jesus came. So the other disciples told him, "We have seen the Lord!"
But he said to them, "Unless I see the nail marks in his hands and put my finger where the nails were, and put my hand into his side, I will not believe it."
A week later his disciples were in the house again, and Thomas was with them. Though the doors were locked, Jesus came and stood among them and said, "Peace be with you!" Then he said to Thomas, "Put your finger here; see my hands. Reach out your hand and put it into my side. Don't be unbelieving, but believing."
Thomas said to him, "My Lord and my God!"
Then Jesus told him, "Because you have seen me, you have believed; blessed are those who have not seen and yet have believed."
John 20,24

The amount and weight of proof (signs) is directly proportional to your own needs. Therefore, those who either lack materially or spiritually, if they seek, will find sooner than the others. Is this unfair? Not at all. It is not about rules, how it may appear at first sight. The ones who need more simply believe more, because they really **need** to be. It is not only about wanting (ego) to have "as well". If they believe more, they will get more.

"Therefore consider carefully how you listen. Whoever has will be given more; whoever does not have, even what he thinks he has will be taken from him."
Luk 8,18

This was said in the sense of faith. Yes, faith in God, but who was that God? In fact, it was he himself. Everyone is God to themselves. If you do not use these statements for manipulation (with the help of fear, of course), then everything that is connected with God, is connected with the presence. Then, the one who has faith in the power of presence, will receive, the one who does not, will have it taken from him. Who gives and takes here? It is not a punishing god and his commandments, but in fact you, yourself. Everyone will give himself – by letting himself enjoy. By giving up thoughts, by not dealing with the future or the past, but living in the presence. Like this, he will let himself enjoy everything. If not, he will be engrossed in thinking when perhaps looking at a beautiful flower. He will be engaged with worries which happened or will "definitely" happen. The flower will forgive him because it has faith in itself, in infinite life. It will forgive him because he does not know what he is doing. He is under the power of present creatures. He will be living his hell on earth. His worst fears will come true. Fear that burns inside will realize itself on the outside. Vice versa, the one who believes will enjoy every moment more and more. He will give and receive even more. He will give because he will have. Do you think that only a fool can do it, a simple minded person? That is what it's all about, to be free of the mind's governance.

"Blessed are the poor in spirit, for theirs is the kingdom of heaven."
Mat 5,3

Do not attach to anything what anyone says about you. Do not judge yourself through the eyes of others. Do not deal with too many things. There is only one thing that matters really. What you feel matters; where you are from the position of faith in yourself.

Here, I will explain another quotation:

"If anyone wants to sue you and take your shirt, let him have your coat as well."
Mat 5,40

This is the quotation that the mind and many others are against. It is because they still do not want to understand it. What is meant by this? If you give up everything, you are enlightened. If we presume that you have been walking along the path of truth, love and life, because this is addressed to you, you are determined to do so. Everyone is your teacher, a teacher for self- knowledge. Yes, absolutely everyone. The neighbor that has gossiped about you, the beautiful girl you meet in the bakery every morning and the homeless person in front of the super-market who stares at you. All these people hold a mirror up to you.

How do they teach you? We will show it by using this quotation. If you are free of all forms of fear, then you do not attract anything negative. There is no dark contained in light. This means that it will not (in your life) happen that someone will take your "shirt" from you. Unless you are not so strong in your faith, but how do you find this out? How do you find out in what phase of the transformation of consciousness you are? The world, as a mirror, serves you for this purpose. You meet people who hold your mirror up to you. The closer the people are to you, the sharper the image is. Sure, it can be more painful – such a direct look into the eyes of the truth. Your "neighbors" are the ones who give you the answer to the question – what is your situation like. Therefore, isolation (asceticism, a cloistered life) is nonsense. It can be reasonable for a while, but as a life intention, it would only be about sacrifice. Sacrifice is neither the sense of life nor God's will. How do we understand the above statement? If someone took your "shirt", then you were not fully conscious, free of fear. Give him also your "coat", as a reward for an enormous gift (compared to whatever price of "the shirt") he has given you. It is a reward for the information about your weak points (even the well hidden ones) which you still have. It can seem foolish now, but I am not speaking about the beginning of the journey when you are only now uncovering the truth. I am talking about more distant places where such information is the most valuable (the only thing that matters).

Then, you will perceive absolutely differently, if you lose something. You will get much more by the act itself and also later – thanks to the understanding you will reach. One of the reasons to give up "your shirt" is to accept the situation and the information that the situation contains. The second reason why to give even more – "the coat" is the fact that to realize the gift (information) fully, you need to pay for it; in any way, to donate something (to maintain the balance of energies), to also give away your "coat". Once you give it to someone needy – he would not want to take it from you if he would not need it (turn away the cold=fear), but above all, you will maintain the energy balance. **It is like the coin for the ferryman.** Remember the chapter where we spoke about the difference in potentials and what is energetically more convenient. Because you have innately (maybe absurdly according to you) created the need to prove in which phase of consciousness you are in, you created a certain decompression which had drawn the particular situation which would have not occurred otherwise. The situation occurred because you had too little faith in yourself. You needed an answer. So, you got it. Not God, you had given the answer to yourself. It means that you needed what had happened, nobody hurt you (like ego supposed), only your will has been fulfilled. The difference of potentials had occurred and Existence (God) intervened – found someone who needed the opposite experience. You receive a big gift – information which is: open your eyes! So, if you do not give and do not reward the one who took it from you for giving you (unconsciously, probably) the gift – information about your real state, then you are acting one-sidedly. You will take the information but will

129

not give anything back. Again, disharmony will occur and will be dealt with by an intervention from "the above". Through realizing and giving, you maintain balance. This is the real substance of ancient ("pagan") rituals of offerings.

This happens if you realize it all, if not, you may think it is "an interplay of coincidences". Everything I am describing can be summarized by the saying: "Unhappiness never comes alone". What does this mean? It means that you substantially (at the level of your own being) need to realize something but you again and again do not want to give up and accept it (present creatures very often are behind this and know that they would lose their control over you if you realize the reality). You have been struggling over and over and therefore, you have been suffering strokes of misfortune. Some people are able to realize (stop thinking) only in the face of death e.g. in a hospital after a serious injury. People often change their opinions and values there, don't they? But they usually forget quickly after they leave the hospital.

I will describe a hypothetical example of your possible future. Imagine that you are on the path of transforming your consciousness already at a certain distance. Not many situations affect you (not evoke emotions), you have probably changed your job and have also been having a happy relationship. You read interesting books, you already have the skills to choose them yourself. You differentiate between facts and hypothesis. You sometimes even communicate with present creatures. It seems that everything is in harmony. You no longer have the health problems that troubled you some time ago. Although you sometimes feel a little unease, somewhere deep down, like a vibration. You are not sure if it is not an illusion. Suddenly, the situation of "the shirt" and "the coat" occurs. Do you understand how happy you will be in that moment? Thanks to your state of consciousness you will be able to perceive the whole situation differently (similarly to what I have described) and know what it really means. You will be redeemed. The place of disharmony in you will be uncovered for you. You need a teacher up to a certain phase, then life, God, will be your teacher. It is you – your own being who will lead you. You are on the edge of the mind and the soul. You are not worried, you have come to the first state of unity of the body (the mind) and the soul (the own being).

When I speak about giving up, it is the first important step on the way to the transformation of consciousness. Surrender is important from both the intangible and tangible point of view, giving up oneself from the point of importance. → *Meditate on this*

Importance is a manifestation of ego and if you do not surrender, you will not get beyond a certain point. You may not feel this limit immediately but once you stop there, it will stop you. Then it will be complicated to uncover what has blocked you from going further. By developing yourself, present creatures change their method of influencing you. This method becomes more and more sophisticated. It is given by their need, by their functional part. If they would have only wanted it, it would not be functional. It works properly because they really need it. Otherwise, they die (from their point of view). Therefore, at the end of the first phase of the transformation of consciousness you will be persuading and leading your own ego and mind, step by step, to realize the way you yourself are being led now. They will also resist, have their own truths and persuasions, opinions like "No work, no money." or "Money does not grow on trees." and so on. Do not leave anything for later.

Give up your own importance and you will be surprised that you will be getting so much from everywhere. Give up wanting to know everything immediately. You will see that the connections will be suddenly much clearer to you. Let yourself be lead. I am not saying that you should believe to everything you read or hear. On the contrary, discover and try things. But above all, do something because time is running out.

Take back your soul, your power and your faith. Nobody can stop you from doing so. There is only one possible way to salvation and atonement; via presence, from the inside, by the way of the female principle.

New information has not been freely accessible for a long time. Through new scientific (mind) technologies more and more is being unveiled. A simple trick has been used – a needle in a hay stack. There is so much information that the truth is hidden in such a sophisticated way, that it is not possible to recognize it without extra sensory skills. It does not matter, the truth can be hidden but you will find it. At first, in yourself, later anywhere you look. The intention of this book is to uncover some of the truths and illuminate the path which everybody walks by himself.

Give up your own importance, look for humility. Let me use another comparison. If you are sitting at a big table as a guest, do not occupy the most honorary place next to the host. You do not know who else is coming. How would you feel if the host asked you to give up your place

Lose Yourself = Freedom ♥

for someone else? It's better to give up your own importance and sit humbly further down. The host will then
come to you and invite you to the honorary place next
to him. How will you feel when you walk towards him
passing by the others? It has been written: "The one who
puts himself higher will be humiliated and the one who
is humble will be put higher." The sense is not, as many
wrongly think, to humiliate yourself the way we understand this today but to give up your importance, your
mask, your role, position. Not to radiate your haughty
opinion of yourself. That you are "somebody" because
you are rich, have status, influence, an education etc.
This is snobbery because all these fragments exist only
"thanks" to their opposites – the poor and the powerless.
Do not deal with the problems of others, deal with yourself. If you have only a little seed of real faith, you will do
miracles.

We have said that salvation (atonement, the path) leads
through the presence, through the Son – Jesus Christ.
When I mentioned Jesus of Nazareth, I pointed out the indication – Jesus Christ. Now we will explain this in detail.

The indication "Christ" is a certain legacy, not only to
Christ as the Messiah, but a direct connection to crucifixion, to the cross. We can find it in the Greek letter
"chi", which is written like an "X" (Christos = Christ).
The legacy to the cross turned the way we have already
spoken about. If you sense Jesus as the presence, for
emphasizing the presence, he is placed on the cross
(a symbol) but differently than you may think. It is
again about using the symbol of the Trinity. This time,
the trinity of symbols – Jesus himself, the centre of the
cross (place and time of this reality) and the placement

10/10/13 · You are not free, you are identifying
yourself with things. Observe
the strategy!! *(ego.)*

of Jesus' s body on the cross. This is the symbol which is a symbol in a symbol. At most crosses, Jesus is shown already tortured and dead, hanging from the nails that are spiked into his hands. This is the symbol of the mind – that to the mind this being is not understandable. The key is in extra sensory perception (female method), thanks to which you can decipher this code. If you examine the symbology of the position of Jesus on the cross, his head is placed at the centre of the cross; the main field of the mind, but also of the sixth gate. That is why this symbol can be understood using extra sensory perception. This is further supported by the symbol of crossed feet. The crucifixion is symbolized most frequently this way. But you can also find symbols where Jesus is alive. And this is exactly what we are talking about. Jesus is placed at the cross in the position where in the middle of the cross is the main cross of his body – whose centre is the fourth gate (chakra), the field of eternity, infinity and love. Through this symbol his message was supposed to be passed on for eternity. This symbol is often emphasized by the position of Jesus's feet that are nailed next to each other – equality of the male and the female principle in creation. Because Jesus Christ is love, infinite and eternal.

Have you not seen such a cross? You can see it for example in Prague in St. Vitus Cathedral, in the area of the Prague Castle. You can already see it above the entrance to the church.

Although, by intervention of the church controlled by the male principle, the symbol of suffering of Jesus tortured and dead, was spread most widely. Paradoxically, this is the symbol of the victory of the mind.

Jesus's message has remained alive, the Holy Grail has been releasing its mysteries hidden in symbols and words. Notice in how many places the aspect of the female principle is hidden.

The crucified Jesus, the symbol of crucifixion, will unveil one more mystery to us. If you divide the human body into two halves – upper and lower, then the upper one is the male principle and the lower one is the female principle. The upper part, the body at the cross, we clarified above. We will now look at the lower part, Jesus's feet!

Feet played a certain role already during Jesus's life, during his public actions. Remember how Mary Magdalene was washing his feet, treated them with aromatic salve and dried them with her hair. Some of the inter-

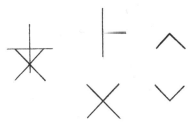

The symbol of the male and the female aspect of the human body represented by the cross in two positions.

pretations clarify this as the symbol of his coronation, anointment by femininity (the rulers had been appointed by the anointment of the head). This aspect, which was later symbolized by christening, had, in the female aspect, appeared earlier at Jesus's contemporary, John the Baptist (who symbolizes the early Christian Buddha, the innate part, femininity). John the Baptist baptized with water, the female principle (information). It is not a coincidence that he was beheaded (the centre of the mind – the male principle) by the order of King Herod. What is this about? This is the precise question. The key is in the word; in the word "**to go**". "Go" contains many hidden meanings. Above all, it is about movement, the manifestation of life. Going symbolizes the path. Our presence on the path we walk. Is it starting to be clearer? Walking (going) is connected with understanding, grasping – owning in the sense that you identify with something that becomes a part of you. For example in the statement that **two people are going out together**. It is not only about that they go together but, above all, that **they have a mutual path**. At the same time, it is important to perceive that **they walk next to each other** (not behind each other). If you are "going out" together then you "are" together. The question "Who are you going out with now?" is the same as "Who are you with now?" The presence (are) is obvious here and also respect and humility (next to each other, at eye level). There is one more metaphor: "Who are you sleeping with now?" "To sleep with somebody" has many meanings. We will look at this in more detail in the chapter about sex. Notice how the aspect of the word going (walking) is being used. We say: "It is going well." "I need to get the company up and running". "I need to get the computer going."

What is "going" connected with? With the feet, of course. **Feet enable us to walk**. Maybe you have met someone who has said that he can learn better at school if he can walk there. Some people say that they meditate when they run. Why? If you run, you activate the body much more than if you sit in front of a computer or the TV, for example. You know that the mind is directly connected with the body and if it has to control the body then it does not have as much energy for "thinking". So, if you run freely then the mind achieves harmony in such a way that it can work partially, but not to think over and over (an endless process without a result). Then, you can use the mind naturally. It does not have so much capacity that it could take control (decision making, the final word) because it also controls all the processes in the body. The faster you run the more the body needs its attention and there is no room left for thinking. Here is the magic of having "a clear head" after doing sports. If you run freely, your mind is in harmony with the body (the opposite state is when you sit at the computer and think about something over and over). If you run as fast as possible, then thinking is simply impossible. Then the body uses the mind fully. It does not mean that you will not get any idea, the other way around. After some kind of endurance, you will have open perception and communication via the soul (as when you are falling asleep). We can call this inspiration or vision. Try it, you will be surprised.

These are natural processes. When they are angry, people say they need to walk a bit. Walking (running), like meditation, use the feet as its ears, it listens to the gentle vibrations of the Mother Earth. **Feet hear the Earth**. It is again the female way; intuitive, extra sensory, intangible and inspirational. That is why women like walking barefoot. They sense their connection more intensely, like children do. Do not forbid children to walk barefoot, you would destroy their natural connection with the Earth, the mother of creation.

You can intensify this experience when walking in water (Jesus walked on water), if you walk barefoot on morning dew. Just try it. It is about the connection of the body with earth, legs – feet with earth. You already know that we have identified the energy gates (chakras) on the human body. There are reflexive points at the feet which correspond to the particular gates of the body. Thanks to this connection, the feet are a substantial part of the human body (in other words, as I said before, everything in the human body is equally important, it is only about whether you have enough "information").

Jesus himself washed the feet of his disciples. This act, again, has many meanings. Perceive it now as the act through which Jesus was harmonizing the energy system (chakras) of his followers, enabling them to be in unity, innately. By touching their feet, he passed "power" and faith that became a part of them. Because he had done it through touching their feet, we can again find here a sign of the female principle.

While walking, feet have much greater significance then you may have thought. You may know the symbology of starting on the right foot, which comes from hidden Masonic teachings. Freemasons (builders of the temple of humanity) also distinguish ways of walking according to their position in the system (sanctification). Walking, changing the left leg (the female principle) and the right leg (the male principle) fulfills existence and significance of both the principles in creation – this is what movement represents and symbolizes. Notice that if animals need to move extremely fast, then they do not change the left and right foot but they move the front and the back legs at the same time.

What do the legs of Jesus on the cross symbolize to us? His feet are crossed in the shape of the cross "X", the nail is spiked into the area that corresponds with the fourth gate and with the position of Jesus himself on the middle of cross which has the shape "+". His left leg in under the right one, the female principle is inside and the male is outside.

The End of the First Chapter

Work with emotions is the essential skill leading to the transformation of consciousness. You will encounter this repeatedly during your journey. Do not underestimate this skill, and practice it in every situation. You can discuss in detail how to swim in water but you cannot learn how to swim out of water. Therefore, work with emotions right in the moment when the emotion is coming or you are experiencing it. You cannot deal with emotion if you are in peace or just thinking about it. Do enjoy every situation where you can practice this "swimming". Gradually, along wih successful practice, you will stand out of the System. Not every present creature will hit you. These actions (attacks) will be passing by you more and more. You will be observers, you will stand away. Not above or under, you will stand next to the System at eye level...

Gospel of Thomas:
Jesus says: "Become passers-by."
Thomas 42

Children

We will be talking about children because the development that a human being (a child) undergoes in its childhood has a direct influence on the rest of their life. You were once also a child.

※ Childhood is also the first part that we will be dealing with after grasping the principles of working with emotions. It is the first point of the Holy Trinity from the viewpoint of energy centres of the human body (see the third part of the book), the connection of the first and the seventh chakras, the relationship of the mother and the father. Their relationship manifests directly in a child's life and forms a child both physically (the body) and mentally (the soul).

We will deal with the development of the human being from the phase of embodiment. Human beings are influenced by what is happening around them already from this point. Who says or does what, how the father treats the mother and the other way around. The first problems may have their beginning here, especially with so-called unwanted children. These are mistakes of unconscious parents. It is necessary to beware of such mistakes. If they have already happened, then realize that they are not only your mistakes, but mistakes which you have gained via the unconsciousness of your parents, and they from theirs. It is of no use for you to try to look for whose fault it is. It is necessary to realize all the mistakes and liberate yourself from their influence. This is possible at any age, and the sooner the better.

I will describe some fundamental moments that influence the development of a human being. Realize yourself what happened when you were a child.

In the mother's body, the new human being goes through the whole development of the physical form on this planet. This is necessary for realization of the own position. The own being (soul) is present in the body already during this time and learns from the mother how to react to different impulses. This is a very important period. Although the body is not, especially in the beginning, very similar to a human, the own being is already present. **The child is fully conscious and his existence in the presence is perfect**. Consequently, the own body is being created and is influenced by outside factors and the need to realize himself, to be born, comes. Already in this phase it is obvious whether the relationship which the child is coming into is harmonious or not. The human being comes into the world exactly at the right time. It does not come too early or too late, the child comes in the moment that he needs for his own development. Right after birth, the child is very vulnerable. **Father should always be present at the birth.** As the mother herself is physically involved in the last phase of the physical (tangible) birth (realization) of the child to this reality, the father is involved in the last phase intangibly. Birth is the act of the male principle in a woman that divides and gives birth (creates). Therefore, the father's presence (the presence of the part of his female principle) **irreplaceably** completes the unity of creation.

The father's presence at the birth gives a message to the child: "You are here as you should be. **Both of us** are waiting for you. Everything is one, complete and in unity, in harmony."

The hands of the father are the first hands that hold the baby after the birth and immediately hand over the baby to the mother. The baby feels presence and protection (acceptance) from the father and then the mother's acceptance which is manifested by putting the baby to her breast. This way the essential communication between mother and child is started (changed), replacing the communication through the umbilical cord. As the new way of communication (breastfeeding) is "going on", it is necessary to let the original way of communication (through the umbilical cord) naturally run its course and not to rush with cutting it.

Look at the conditions in which births have been handled in the last 50 years, it's no surprise that there are so many people with emotional problems.

If your reality does not correspond to the above description in any way, then search for the answers to your questions anywhere that they diverge.

Breastfeeding is one of the most important forms of communication between the baby, the mother and the environment that surrounds them. We will stop here for a while:

Jesus turning to women, said:
"Weep not for me, but weep for yourselves, and for your children. For behold, the days are coming in which they will say: 'Blessed are the barren, the wombs that never bore, and the breasts that never nursed.'"
Luk 23,28

Despair is mirrored in this statement where society is so wrong and so far from its nature, when it dictates that it is "absolutely fine" if women do not breastfeed or even give birth at all; that it's all right to care more about their "work", their looks and so on.

Look at breastfeeding in your childhood. Step by step, the era of milk and baby artificial formula based on milk is coming to an end. Realize, from the energy-information point of view, what cow milk gives to a baby. In cow milk, there is only information about what it is, a cow. Here is the basis of the tendency of people, who were fed by cow milk, to create flocks. These children were pushed to receive cow milk as nutrition, and on top of that – instead of mother's (human) milk!

Explanations saying that cow milk contains some nutritional substances which the baby needs are absolute nonsense. In the time of Communism in Eastern bloc countries, this method of "nursing" was so widespread that people thought (older generations still think so!) that to breastfeed (more than a couple of months) is unnatural, not normal, maybe even harmful for a woman. Here seek for the origin of your control by present creatures, that it is possible (and frankly said, so easy) to control you. Who else could be standing in the back of such an absurd thing – to nurse a human being with cow (or any other) milk? It has been the work of a present creature that with the help of the mind (science) – the male principle (external, dividing). The state when you give control of yourself so easily is, apart from others, caused by absolutely incorrect information that you received when you were children. One of the first and the most substantial things is insufficient breastfeeding by the mother. Therefore, you feel so dissatisfied, whatever you do, sooner or later the feeling will come – dissatisfaction.

You were not given what you should have been given. You were not satisfied – given appropriate food. Instead of mother's (human) milk you were given cow's milk. You were not nursed enough by your mother. It is not about some nutritional substances at all, as science (medicine) influenced by the mind keeps saying. Breastfeeding is a broad-spectrum communication tool. A baby has on the upper palate a place (something like "a sensor") through which he communicates with his mum. In return, a woman has such a place in her nipples. By having a nipple in the mouth, information is being transmitted.

A human being (a baby) does not live from mother's milk. This is the clarification of why babies sometimes want to be fed without external (minds') causes and why they sometimes turn away immediately after they start to suckle. In this moment, it was "only" about communication, an exchange of information between mother and child.

Just as a baby says (through communication with a nipple) what content of mother's milk he needs, the same way the baby gathers information of what is going on. The baby sees that his mother is crying but does not understand why – his current experience is not enough to grasp what is happening. The baby wants to be breast-fed and asks to be brought to the breast. The baby just wants to confirm something. Imagine how the baby feels without such an possibility. How many unanswered questions from the time of infancy remain stored in the subconscious. What about abandoned babies in orphanages.

If you feel, after reading these lines, that something is happening "inside" yourself, then it is a sign that this area of your life has not yet been dealt with. How to reach harmony, again?

Try to realize that you forgive your mother that she did not fully satisfy your biological needs if this is what happened. That is why you feel dissatisfied inside. And if you do already know, do not do this with your own children. If it has already happened, apologize to them. If you do not have enough courage, do it silently in spirit. Repeat your apology as often as you need to. They hear you and need to hear the truth, as you do.

Another fundamental need of a baby is to be literally attached to his mother in the first years of life. We can see this with some indigenous cultures where women have their position and nobody tells them what they should do with their children (especially not men). If you are a woman, perceive your instincts. As mother you know what to do. Just trust yourself. If you are not mother yet, do not be afraid of what will come. You will know what to do, how to take care of your baby. You will always have enough information in the presence. Let yourself know and use extra sensory perception which you, as a woman, have active.

If you are a man, respect your wife. Give advice only if you are asked for it. For you, it will be a spiritual exercise of mastering your ego because who else wants to be right and who else (inside a man) knows best what his wife should or not do, feel or perceive? Your wife will give you more love than your mind can imagine if you respect her. What can an unconscious man know about birth? Even if he was at a thousand births, he could only recognize their external manifestation. This is a male method. He could never know what a woman experiences, feels. Be supportive to your wife, protect her and support her self-consciousness by respecting her decisions. Let her make mistakes. Stand by her, not behind her. Protect her, do not watch her!

Do not blame yourself for anything. Realize that they are only mistakes that come from situations where you simply did not know. Whenever you can set things right, it is never too late.

We have said that the baby should be in close contact with his mother. Especially in the first years of life (the first three years it is the most needed). Women often have the feeling they do not know what they should do with their children, where they should put them. They think that they cannot do this and that because of children. They hand this information over to them (children). How do children feel? It is not such a limitation to have a baby with you, as it may seem at first sight. Indigenous women carry their children in a scarf closely attached to their bodies. Take your baby to you as often as possible. Put your shopping bag in the trolley and carry the baby in your hands, it is better than the other way around.

A woman has the feeling that she must attend to a baby. She needs time for it but she also needs time for housework and other things. This is a substantial mistake. Most of all, the child needs to experience everyday life. Not to be in his "perfect" bedroom and play with "perfect" toys. The sense of his games is to recognize and only recognition can fully satisfy him. What does that mean for a woman (a man)? It means to deal with their usual activities as before. **The baby is not here to limit his parents but to teach them. So that, they can realize!** Be aware how much love your child gives you, how endlessly he trusts you…

If you respect this nature, you will suddenly realize that you do not have less time than before. And on top of that, you enable your child to experience everyday life with you, life the way it is. This is what interests your baby! Your baby came to you because he needs your life experiences. A better father is not the neighbor who plays football with his children in the garden. A better mother is not the neighbor who bakes pastry or organizes children's games all the time. It is you. Your child has chosen you – yourself. Do not judge according to "general" norms which say how things "should" actually be.

Deal with what you need to and have your baby with you. Do not perceive your baby as a limit. He does not perceive you as a limit either, although he could have done so – better than you. Babies live consciously in the presence. They do not sense time and go by the instincts of their body. These are correct.

Imagine you have come to this reality to enjoy and to play this magnificent game. You sense noises, colors, touch and you want more. You want to recognize and unveil. You use your senses through which you can recognize and realize the tangible world. You are ready. Then your frightened mother, who is even afraid to touch you, comes. She went through all the available courses, read all the recommended books. She knows "sudden infant death" syndrome and "she is alert". She equipped your bedroom with the most expensive (so, the best) stuff she could afford. She has not spared money on anything (maybe only on herself, which she might silently blame you for later). She looks at you like at a ghost. She stopped breastfeeding after several weeks, they say it is enough and according to leaflets from the pharmacy artificial nutrition is sufficient. She also does not want to make her breasts unattractive (her husband could find someone else). You have a weird electronic thing under your bed that watches if you are breathing. You are lying in your silent (perfect) bedroom looking at still things around you. It is silent and there is muted light everywhere. The mother is equipped with information that she should not react to any crying, otherwise the baby will be spoilt, she brings her skills to "perfection". After several weeks, she stops breastfeeding and puts her baby to sleep in a separate bedroom. The baby's desperate cry implies that something is wrong, the baby is present and does not understand time. It is necessary to endure, not to enter the baby's room, the high-principled father helps out with this. He knows that the rules must be kept and implanted in the baby from early infancy, otherwise the baby will think he's the boss. The horror of motherhood and childhood starts running at their full extent. Two frightened parents who do not know what is happening and what they should do, following external information (the male principle). The baby starts to slowly but surely learn from this and gradually realizes that it is possible to get closer to the parents through illness. He learns how to create chronic diseases which put him back in the proximity of the parents, into his mother's arms. He needs to be touched, cuddled, so various types of eczema follow.

What to do about this? Be aware that it is natural that the baby expects to experience your everyday work. If the baby can share it with you, it will be much better for him than if you reserve two hours per day especially for him, during which you attend to him "fully". The baby perceives your inner dissatisfaction when you play with him instead of finishing work that you are supposed to do. The baby cannot explain this to himself other than it is his fault and the feeling of guilt takes over. This is a mistake. Cuddle your baby anytime he needs it.

Respect your baby and do not expect anything. Especially, do not anticipate what he will be like, what he will or will not do, how he will behave in a particular situation. Treat him as a welcomed guest. Consider your baby as your equal. If you do not do so, you take his divine substance away from him. This is the reason why god is separated from people, from the male principle point of view. This is the reason why people do not perceive themselves as gods, as a part of him. In the past, children were treated as inferiors. They were not respected. You transfer similar principles of behavior to your children. Do realize this!

The parent knows of course better than the baby when the baby should eat. He knows what the baby likes and how much he should eat. When he is supposed to go the bathroom, what the excrement should look like, what is the right amount, when and how he should be sleeping, when he should wake up and so on. What or whom he should play with. Although there is so much we can learn from children all the while.

✱ *"For he who is least among you all is the one who is great."*
Luk 9,48

Recall how limiting it was for you when you were treated the way described above, at home, in kindergarten or at school. Remember and realize how you felt. You have the power to stop this curse. To stop it for yourself, for your children, for everyone who is involved.

A duty is connected with this – you must do something. If you must do something, it is not unconditional acceptance at all. If you are in the space of unconditional acceptance, you do not have to do anything. It is the same with children. Guide your children naturally – by the way of needs, not by conditions and orders.

The big fault is not to answer if a child asks something, or to say something foolish, just to say anything.

Be aware of the fact that a child is the best teacher you can ever have. It is a wonderful experience if you accept it. The child deals with you naturally at eye level. Many parents and especially grandparents perceive this as a lack of respect. The child neither puts himself up nor undermines himself.

✗ *"See that you do not despise one of these little ones."*
Mat 18,10

If you talk to a child, communicate at eye level. Sit or kneel down on the floor. Do not look at him from above nor take him up to yourself, he then loses the solid earth under his feet, loses the contact with the Mother Earth.

Our relationship with our children is influenced by our relationship with our own parents. This is a very sensitive topic. Many people do not get over it and this is exactly the problem. People are constantly searching for methods of how to get around this topic, so that they do not have to deal with it. They pace between various spiritual systems or they close themselves into some dogma. They are continuously searching for the right way that they won't have to deal with the relationship with their parents. They solved it a long time ago, of course, and if a therapist tells them something different, then they think that he "had pulled out" the proven topic because he did not know what to do with their problems.

The theme of parents – children is substantial. It is the first point of the Holy Trinity, the connection of the first and the seventh chakras, mother and father. The most solid geometric shape is the triangle. In connection with parenthood, imagine the relationship of parents and a child as a triangle where on the tops are the mother, father and child. If the relationship with one of the parents is, for any reason, different than with the other parent, then an imbalance occurs.

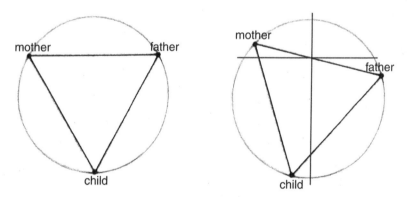

The triangle manifests the relationship between a child and his parents. If the relationships are harmonious, the triangle is in balance. If any top of the triangle wants to get closer or further from the neighboring top, imbalance and disharmony occur. There can be only one representative (one child, one mother and one father) on each top.

If you want to walk through this and close the door of the past behind you, then there is no other way than to balance the relationship with your parents. Only this way, you will gain both parts of the first "seal" that opens the past. Without dealing with the past it is much harder to go further.

Every child has his own triangle with his parents. There are more triangles in families with more than one child. If there are more children (or all of them) on the position of one child in the family, this will cause a damaged self-consciousness and self-confidence of the children. In addition, the relationship between the younger children and parents may change and children may replace this relationship with the relationship to an older sibling. Relationships can become distorted and this will have a substantial influence on the development of an individual.

Every child has his own relationship with both the parents, his own triangle, irreplaceable and incompatible. If parents do not respect this, children (human beings) will have problems with their self-perception, especially, problems with self-consciousness and self-confidence. When reading these lines, realize how it was when you were a child. Let us find the causes in relationships between parents and children.

Therefore, it is necessary to give your full attention to children. Every generation can stop the curse in the form of education. You have the possibility, now is the right moment. Simply trust yourself and your children.

Give up your dependency. Fictitiously needed, but in fact nonsensical. Do not make your children dependent on you. How? By not living your dependency through your children. This is a problem, especially with mothers because they have lived a part of their life dependent on their children. When a child leaves, the sense of their life dies. Sometimes, the horror of motherhood is so extreme that lonely forty-year old "children" live with their parents (usually, only with the mother, the father has either left or died). They hate each other and suffer from feeling guilty. Mutual guilt. It is possible to interrupt it if you realize the situation and continue discovering what influenced you when you were a child. **The key to the many gates of consciousness is forgiveness**. Only through forgiveness, can you release the accumulated and closed energy of feelings (or emotions) from your body. How? Just like that, by deciding to do it. No rituals, maybe only a short verbal formula of what you are doing at the moment, something like: **"I forgive myself. I forgive them. They forgive me."**

Most of the time the theme of the relationship between parents and children is so deeply locked up that it is very difficult to open it without being in the presence of a therapist (but it is possible). The universal truth is, in this case, the same as many times before, it is necessary to get balance and harmony. To discover the difficult situation, which caused the disharmony, and to grasp it, understand it (accept it by the mind) and "the magic" is in forgiving. Not to dwell on the past and not to experience your hurt over and over, to find the power to forgive even great injuries. In my practice, I meet with very moving experiences of my clients from their childhood. **Forgiveness is the narrow gate to enlightenment** which you cannot walk through if you do not release the past which you drag with you. To release it means to forgive.

We have stated that embodiment is the intended conscious act when we, as own beings, determine a place. You know then, what you are stepping into, it is enough if you realize this. In this reality, the aim (the sense of the actual game) is to experience. If we use religious language, God (as if standing somewhere "away" from this reality) created this world and all its connections. Now, he comes through human beings to experience the miracle of creation.

The task of every person is to experience, discover and create. With this awareness, we come into this reality. In the moment of embodiment, when the soul enters the body of the embryo, there is such a powerful first experience that all other information, which we carry to this reality, is completely drowned out. The wide-spectrum perceptions, perceived by the "newly" embodied human being are so fascinating for him that it shadows all the rest, also the awareness of the human being himself. The being experiences a whole development, all the experiences are coded into the DNA of the body. This happens roughly until the half point of the pregnancy. It is a magnificent story, which is so interesting that we can compare it with watching a movie in the cinema, where all of a sudden you "forget" about your job tasks (for example) and you become a part of the story that you are watching. The human embryo goes through the complete development of biological forms on this planet. Because the soul and the body are in unity at this moment, the particular phases are at the same time both intangible and tangible (the embryo really changes its features according to the state of development in which he is at the moment).

The emergence of a person starts in the moment the sperm meets the egg in a women's body. The body of human beings has evolved this way for all eternity. Development is from a cell into a person. Birth is not the beginning of development – that has been going on for a long time.

Now we are speaking about the human body which, as we said, is one of the substances of a human being (the other two are the own being and the spirit). The body is the physical container in reality. The body has its instincts gained through evolutionary development, its inborn intelligence and skills. The body also has a connector with the own being –the soul. This connector between the tangible body and the intangible own being is the mind. The mind as the connector is able to make assumptions, analyses, is able to communicate both ways, and is materialized first and foremost in the brain. As the brain of the newborn develops, the mind's ability to control the body strengthens. This way, the development phase of a child when he learns how to function in tangible reality, is given. This means that the child starts to control his senses. Sight, hearing, touch, smell and taste. Senses create an imaginary border between tangible reality and intangible reality. In the beginning, when the individual is in harmony, they use all the senses equally. This is the time when the baby, from the parents' point of view, puts everything into his mouth. Parents do not like to see this. Their controlled minds see everything as a potential source of infection and other negative influences. This period, an oral phase, is nothing extraordinary. Only adults have taste exclusively connected with food. That is why they first notice this projection which does not correspond with their ideas of correct contact with the outside world. Using the other four senses is all right with them, so they let the baby be. Later, when adults think that the baby understands more, they start to forbid him to use the other senses, saying things like: it is not good to touch this, do not look at that, this is not something for your ears, do not sniff that, you are not a dog and so on.

Gradually, the child is influenced and domestication begins. The present creatures which control the parents prepare other sheep from the children for themselves. Parents voluntarily, together with a feeling of "correctness" bring up their children in the way which society, led by science (controlled by present creatures via the mind), considers to be the right one. Mothers entirely controlled (without their own freedom) go to see pediatricians or psychologists and ask them how they should bring up their children, how to understand and know them. **The biggest possible paradox occurs**. Mother – a woman, who knows best from nature how to take care of her child, asks someone else, a strange man (a doctor, a psychologist) what she should do…

The baby – a full-valued human being who learns how to use his body, discovers himself and outer reality through the body senses and does not fully understand what is going on here.

The baby does not understand why adults do not perceive anything else than what they can perceive via the senses of their bodies. He has his own way of communication – crying and body reactions. We have gotten used to calling some of these reactions illnesses. These are natural reactions that mothers know and can react to if they are conscious, and are not blind and controlled.

The reality is that the horror, which the baby has to go through, the horror which cause the parents (by good will), will influence the new human being so much that he will be partly or entirely functionless; enslaved.

Everything starts in the mother's body. Mothers are not aware that everything that influences them directly influences their baby. Now, we will focus mainly on intangible vibrations. The tangible influence, the physical influence of the embryo in the mother's body, is clear.

From the viewpoint of intangible frequencies, it is mostly about the feelings that the mother experiences. Usually one of the first feelings is surprise – either "pleasant" or "unpleasant". This is the first impulse which, at an intangible level, the own being coming into the "body" of the embryo perceives. Now, I will be talking about "you", for reasons of better comprehension of the text, but please, do not take it personally.

Take the following description as figuratively as the creation of the world by god represented by a wise old man sitting on a cloud. The description, although it is on purpose, corresponds with the truth.

You come into "the world" and an agreement precedes it, something like a sacred agreement with the own beings of your mother and father. You ask them for your body. You have chosen them. Their combination perfectly fits your intention here in this reality; the combination of the father's DNA and the mother's DNA. The connection of their bodies is exactly what you need and what will enable you to experience what you need to experience. You contact them and ask for permission. It is the direct communication which an individual can perceive, a woman above all, but it is not like that in most cases today. The parents agree and conception, accompanied by intercourse as the tangible part, takes place. In this moment, when your intention to embody is tangibly realized, you enter this reality. For now, the human being is not yet "anchored" in himself. The consistency of the soul and the newly created body secures the third substance – spirit, something like "the divine will to be", which manifests fully at the moment of a functional blood system of the embryo.

But you have one piece of information, and that is that you did not come uninvited, that you are here "rightly". Therefore, it is a blow below the belt for you if your parents are surprised that you are here. Your mother is shocked when she finds out at the toilet (used a pregnancy test) that she is pregnant. Why is she wondering, since you have asked her before and she agreed? She even feels it deep down inside, she knows that you have come into her body. Is it possible she has forgotten? How should you feel now? She perceives you as an invader in her body. She observes herself in the mirror and sees it as some kind of drawback. You can perfectly feel her feelings of confusion, fear and uncertainty. Another shock comes from the father when the mother tells him what she has found out: "Are you sure?" What is it to be "sure"? You wonder. The idea of certainty or uncertainty is as unknown to you as the idea of time. The father rejects his participation on this "project". "I don't want this baby, is it even mine?" The mother cries. The father feels pushed into something that he does not want, does not understand and rejects to believe it, he is afraid. He does not want his current life to be taken away from him. Because this is what will definitely happen after the baby is born. You do not understand what is going on. Why are they behaving like this? You have made an agreement. They are only supposed to teach you how to use your body, to show you this reality. You do not want to take anything from them. The mother goes to see a doctor. What is that? You find yourself in the presence of a strange obsessed being. You sense the mother's fear and nervousness. You are not interested in being there. Does the mother not feel this? More and more situations confirm that you are definitely not being accepted.

Here is the beginning of other problems; the lack of unconditional acceptance by the mother and the father.

You try to communicate but most of the time without any results. The more you try, the more the mother is confused and seeks advice from someone else. Your attempts to communicate are perceived by the mother and her surroundings as hormonal changes, various psychosis and so on.

If all chances of communicating with the mother in an extra sensory way have failed, only the chance of sensory communication remains. For the baby it is, most of all, crying and natural body language. Both of these have been (and still are) mostly perceived as something that is not normal.

The baby knows exactly what he needs. His perception is absolutely different from the perception of an adult (who is influenced). The basic difference is in that the baby is entirely conscious and fully present. He has extra sensory access to all information which he does not consider as extraordinary. He does not understand why the parents are so strongly influenced by the mind. The baby does not understand the sense of time nor grasp the idea of "good" and "bad". He is still aware of the fact that his entrance to this reality was a result of an agreed decision of all those involved. Thanks to instinct and natural body intelligence, he starts "to live" and function in tangible reality. He breathes and starts to discover his senses. Step by step, he recognizes that apart from the senses, other ways of sensation are "not really accepted" in this reality. The baby perceives other beings that inhabit this reality but are not embodied. Perceiving them is absolutely equal to the perception of tangible processes by the five senses. Later, when he learns how to speak, he will even talk about it. He does not understand why the adults are playing that weird game that they do not know. They pretend they do not know and let themselves be controlled and used. They behave totally incomprehensibly. By some incomprehensible key, they have split themselves into two groups, the ones who "know" and the ones who "do not know". But the child realizes that neither side knows the truth. The group of those who allegedly know, says nonsense to the others – and they pretend that they believe it. All the while, everyone is unhappy but they pretend they aren't. They destroy their bodies by emotions which is for a baby an unknown frequency. According to the baby, they are doing this consciously (and this is in fact the truth). The baby does not differentiate between conscious and unconscious behavior, this will be "learned" from the parents later...

The child begins to assimilate. Instinctively, he is able to perceive the frequency of love. This is a vibration of the fourth chakra, the frequency of the substance of existence. This is the reason why the baby seeks the mother's (father's) embrace. He needs to have his centre of love in physical contact with their centre of love. The baby instinctively expects that he will be accepted and his needs will be satisfied. These are the primary instincts and needs of the body.

One of the original needs is to be in the mother's presence. It is a completely mistaken opinion that the baby does not understand anything and it is necessary to isolate him from the outside world, so that "nothing wrong happens to him", that is distorting for the baby. On the contrary, the baby's inborn need is to be with the parents – in their presence at all times; to be present during all processes that influence the parents – light, noise, warmth or cold, to learn from them physically and also mentally, by observing their reactions to impulses and to imitate them. This is a natural instinct and a need of the body, and so it is possible to "deform" the baby completely. Much later, the child learns to use and understand the terms of "good" and "bad" and because these are not natural terms, he can "put" in them any model of behavior. For example, if fanaticized by a religious doctrine, the child is able to hurt others in the name of "rightness". Parents influence everything.

Let's go back to the baby. Before I became a father, I did not understand how it was possible to recognize a newborn baby only by his cry. In the moment that I heard "my" baby crying, I understood immediately. The vibration of the newborn baby's voice is something like a finger print. It is absolutely unmistakable for the parents. Whenever I heard "my" baby crying, the instincts of my body were immediately awakened. I woke up immediately once again. My perception was brighter and faster. Suddenly, I felt like if everything around me had slowed down and

I had sped up. All the feelings had the same basis – it was necessary to do something! Because of entirely insufficient education and information in this area and a lack of conscious examples, doubts came immediately. What to do? What remained of the body instincts, after the deformation by education and studies, was only enough for activation of the body. Natural information about what to do had overshadowed the mind with dogma.

The absolute majority of new parents have the same problems. In this regard, the role of the mother, who is from the very beginning physically closer to the baby than the father, is very important. The father however should not undermine his presence and especially not the influence of his feelings to the feelings of the mother and the baby. The fact that the father does not breastfeed, does not mean that he is taken out of the process of influencing his baby from the beginning.

As I have already stated, the baby does not perceive time. If he is abandoned, he does not know if this state will ever end. The baby does not know whether this state can finish at all, that it is a temporary state, not a final (infinite) state. Therefore, an abandoned baby, if he needs its mother's (or his father's) presence at the moment, experiences this respite as definite and his reaction is, therefore, absolutely reasonable. The reaction of the irritated and desperate mother is something like: "Why are you crying so much? I'll be back in a minute." is inadequate. The baby lives in the presence. The mother is either there or she isn't. Hoping or expectations are not familiar to the baby at all. If he needs the mother and she is not with him or her, then the baby calls the mother by crying which is the most natural way.

You also cry if you are not satisfied. You cry because you do not know what to do. All your education and experience are worth nothing, it does not change the situation that you are experiencing. You are at your wit's end (the mind is at its wit's end). What is underneath the mind? Instinct is. What is the first instinct of sensory communication apart from touch? Crying is. So, you cry, in fact you are calling your mother. You need hugs. For sure, you must know that.

The problem is that you as an adult claim to know – better than the baby – what the baby needs and when they need it. This is of course nonsense. This nonsense is strongly supported by systems such as medicine, education etc. Everybody knows what is right for you and when is the right time. There are charts which say at what age the baby is supposed to do something or not. When the baby should sit, get up, laugh. If your baby does not do everything according to the charts, he is evaluated as not normal, delayed. So, the baby needs to be examined, treated and so on. What does the baby experience during that? Nobody is interested neither in what baby experiences nor in the reason why it is like that. The baby is broken and it is necessary to repair him, let's call the repairman – the doctor. He knows better than the baby and than his own mother, what is wrong and how to get it right.

The baby has learned not to trust himself but to trust someone else. The problem, later called a lack of self-confidence, starts to arise. **The baby loses self-confidence.** He is persuaded (by his own mother) that he does not function properly, that his body does not correspond with the expected state. The baby is pushed out of balance of the own being and the physical body. The baby is pushed to an imbalance of his own physical body, to an imbalance of the mind that starts being controlled by present creatures. He does not understand what is going on. He is conscious of himself. He knows that everything is the way it should be, and by the words of the adults, everything is all right. But others see it differently, even his own mother. Without restraint, the baby trusts his mother feelings. She is afraid that something is wrong. The baby has already learned that his mother has "pleasant" feelings if everything is all right. Now he feels that his mother is worried. She is worried that the baby is not all right. The baby is then the cause of the "unpleasant" feelings of its mother... The baby is confused. It knows that everything is the way it should be, he is aware of himself. For the time being. But against what the baby feels, stand the feelings (intangible frequencies) of his mother that say otherwise. These intangible frequencies of the mother's mind are perceived by the developing baby's mind and it identifies with them, he learns. Although the baby was fully conscious, aware of himself, he starts to doubt himself under the pressure of his own mind (of his mother's mind). **The baby loses self-confidence**. In this way, "**listening**" to the voice and to the opinions of others, is being encoded into a new human being. Of course, the most important thing is what others think of you. A person's self-confidence is derived from the reactions of their surroundings. The person gradually becomes dependent on the evaluation of their surroundings.

What message do children bring to us? It is a message of perfection. Their world is present all the time. This is maybe the reason why you sometimes do not understand it. How can a child cry one minute and laugh the next? It is because he is present. Nothing is carried from the past (cry) when joy is being experienced (laugh). Children teach you where to go. They show you the path! Wake up and listen to them!

At that time the disciples came to Jesus and asked, "Who is the greatest in the kingdom of heaven?" He called a little child and had him stand among them. And he said: "I tell you the truth, unless you change and become like little children, you will never enter the kingdom of heaven." Mat 18,2

Listen to yourself, to the child inside you. Uncover what was not satisfied in this child. Satisfy him/her (yourself). Go and play football, break a window, ring bells in the neighborhood. Instead of cigarettes, instead of drugs, buy yourself the toys (which did not exist in time when you were children) you have always wished to have. Play in a sandbox and walk barefoot outside. Paint your body with markers. Run in a storm and pet strange dogs. Ride horses, swim against the current. Do everything you were forbidden to do. If you fill these "blank places" on the map of your childhood, the strange pressure, that you felt inside, will go away. It does not need to be immediate, so do not be impatient, when it comes you will recognize it, you will be sure that it has come.

The last thing I will mention in this part is infertility. If you have this problem, then study the information in the part about the creation of reality in detail. Fertility is connected with creation.

What is influencing you, again, is fear. You can dissolve fear by faith. There is no fear in the presence of faith, as there is no dark in the presence of light…

"Blessed is she who has believed."
Luke 1,45

Sex

"For everything that is hidden will eventually be brought into the open, and every secret will be brought to light."
Mar 4,22

This chapter may be surprising for some of you. I will begin with a fact well known to most of you – sex is a natural biological need of the body. This is not the entire (full) truth. During sex, intercourse, many intangible processes take place. Conception happens through sex, the contact of sperm and an egg in a woman's body (from the physical's body point of view).

We need to unveil and recognize the mystery that sex hides. It is not a coincidence that many churches, religions, spiritual systems and cultural traditions have very concrete attitudes towards sex. Mostly, their attitudes are quite negative or at least very reserved. Family education has not been very good until recent times.

Everything connected with sex was taboo, if not directly forbidden. Masturbation was punished severely in some cultures. The primary sexual relationship is considered to be between a man and a woman. Many cultures have considered women to be unequal, less worthy. The position of women was usually completely undignified. A woman as an object of lust has influenced (attracted) a man at the physical level. In some periods, this was considered to be a weakness (succubus = the sexual demon) and women were accused of being the cause of this "weakness", or even the cause of everything "evil".

Why have there been such taboos about sex?

You already know that we will speak about the second body gate which is determined for working with energies connected to sex, in the sense of creation, movement – change of movement. These are copulation movements (forth and back) that are connected with the symbol itself and with the principles of creation (see the theme about feet and walking). I have been using the term gate instead of chakra on purpose because I perceive it as more convenient (considering the function of the gate).

Now let us look at the context connected with the second body gate in more detail. The second gate (chakra, if you wish) is called the sacral (from the Latin word **sacralis = cross**). Sometimes it is called **the centre of the cross**. Here, the mystery challenges to be unveiled. There is, of course, a connection with the cross. You know that in the middle of the cross, there is the present moment. As we said, it is possible to create only in the presence via the present moment. So, the placement of the gate of creation at the middle of the cross is more than clear. The objection, that the term is not related to the cross as the symbol but it is derived from the sacral bone, is ok. Sure, because this is the cross we are talking about.

From the viewpoint of the human body and its functions, things such as the function of the testicles, ovaries, prostate gland, regulation of the period and the creation of gender are directly related to this gate. From the elements' point of view, the dominant element is water, within the human body it is blood and bodily liquids and also the organs functioning with them, e.g. kidneys, bladder, reproductive organs. Generally, this area is the area of the female principle which also shows the element of water. The mystery of creation is hidden there – in the female principle. That is why a woman gives birth, not the man, although they are both involved equally in creation. The female aspect (in anything) is the biggest mystery that was supposed to be hidden. Gradually, as you become more conscious, you will be able to perceive this information in a wider context. We will now uncover some of the facts.

Water carries information, you already know this. Water carries the old away and brings in the new, water purifies, protects etc. The embryo is surrounded (protected) by water until birth. There are many aspects of water. Water is also magnificent and a wonderful element. You can see it in special constellations of space orbs, when the moon shines, dancing like a fairy near water or seas. Its beauty is not of this world and many sailors could tell stories about it. There are many powers that influence human being which we have not unveiled together yet, this is another one.

It is not a coincidence that sex was damned by many spiritual systems. Whether this attitude was conscious or unconscious is not important anymore. Firstly, it was conscious. From a business point of view, it has always been about information. If information is a tool for manipulation, then it is necessary (from the point of view of power) to hide the source of information. That is a simple truth. Who really reigns? It is the one who knows, the one who has information. It is the same if it is espionage about an army in a foreign country or information on how to control the peoples' minds. It is clear, from this point of view, why sex was rejected. It was about restricting potential contact with information.

Even today, in a period fully controlled by the male principle, we say that we exchange genetic information during sex. Isn't this statement suspicious to you? The deep truth is, again, hidden in this statement. From a logical, sensible (material) point of view, the statement is not true. Only the man gives genetic information to the woman in the form of sperm. A woman does not give anything material to a man. So, the statement about genetic information exchange is not completely right. But during sex, I mean sexual intercourse, information is really transmitted from a man to a woman, and the other way around. This is intangible "genetic" information.

The DNA of the human body is much more complicated than it is publicly acknowledged. If taking a different view (definition), it is even possible to talk about others than currently known structures of both helixes. There are many more helixes. They are directly connected with the energy gates of the human being, with the gates in the body and also outside the human body. A long time ago (at a different place of existence), human beings had been enslaved (see the chapter about God's shepherds). Only two DNA helixes (something like a tangible shell), connected with the first and the second gate, remained transparent in our reality due to these interventions. These two, which are now known, contain information about the physical body (substance) and about the reproductive ability. They are the only ones which were "left" in an open form for human beings, so that people would survive and would be capable (and willing) to let themselves be controlled; create emotion as "food" for present creatures.

172

The ability to sense our own body and the reproductive ability are both limited up to a certain point. Because all the gates are connected in a certain manner and influence each other, it is not possible for some of the gates to be fully functional and others functionless. As you know (see the pictures in the chapter The Mystery of Creation), energy gates (chakras) are altogether directly connected in a certain way. And this will help us to unveil the mystery clarifying why there is so much taboo about sex.

The first gate is connected with the Earth, with the mother, with the physical being on this planet. That is why the embodied human being comes into the world from the mother's womb. The direct interconnection between the first and the seventh gate plays a role here. The connection which could not have been interrupted, because it represents one of the fundamental principles in this reality – the male and the female principle, which only together have the ability to create a new life. This interconnection enables us to also perceive the father, the creator, God (but not so intensely, at the basic level, as the mother). It is him (father) who creates (is active) and gives information to mother (a tangible realization). For the purpose of this connection (a possibility to realize this connection tangibly), the second gate was also left active. Its function is to enable us to experience sex, intercourse, to be present during it, as this is a necessary (the principle, again) part of creation. This is the issue that was necessary to hide. You can realize information only in the presence. You can create only in the presence. You can experience sex only in the presence. But without sex, it wasn't possible to bear children. Therefore, there was a problem – how to let human beings create, to reproduce, which brings the contact with information (in the presence) and at the same time, to restrict potential access to other information which could have taken them (human beings) to a higher consciousness. That is why activity of the energy gates was limited; from the third gate, connected with the mind, up. This third gate has been used to control human beings and its function was influenced. This is the period, which is described in the Bible as the confusion of languages, which allegedly was the punishment for erecting the building that was touching the sky – this building is the comparison of the power that people really have.

But the Lord came down to look at the city and the tower the people were building."Look!" he said. "The people are united, and they all speak the same language. After this, nothing they set out to do will be impossible for them! Come, let's go down and confuse the people with different languages. Then they won't be able to understand each other."
Genesis 11,5 (1st Book of Moses)

The confusion of languages was caused by taking control over this gate and throwing the future down to fear and uncertainty. The third gate is, in fact, directly connected with the fifth gate which is the centre of communication.

Disharmony of these two gates creates the disability to determine the future (the exact placement in existence) which is the third seal of the Holy Trinity (see the part of the creation of reality and about the mystery of creation).

Creation of the future was mastered via fear. Here is the beginning of the powerful, punishing and horrible god.

"You must fear the LORD your God and serve him. When you take an oath, you must use only his name."
Deuteronomium 6,13 (5th Book of Moses)

Through the mastering of the third and (in connection with it) of the fifth gate and also of the third seal of the Holy Trinity itself, humankind was thrown into slavery by present creatures (gods, first of all). If put into simple words, of course.

Let me quote the Bible here again (the Old Testament) for simplicity (also a certain purpose) and an easy understanding of the above stated information.

"O Lord, let your ear be attentive to the prayer of your servant, and to the prayer of your servants who delight to fear your name, and give success to your servant today, and grant him mercy in the sight of this man."
Nehemiah 1,11

Dread and fear in this prayer you can already see yourself. If not clearly, then return to the chapter in which we deal with the word, its power and the analysis of the words "terribly" and "dreadfully".

Let us go back to the second gate (the second chakra). This gate has also its direct interconnection with another gate as we described previously (the first – the seventh and the third – the fifth). It is the interconnection with the sixth gate which is the gate of the extra sensory perception. The function of one gate is directly connected with the function of the other gate. Therefore, if the sexual chakra is functional, a person is sexually active, the sixth chakra is then also functional. This means extra sensory perception. Then, only a little step to realize this reality remains to be taken. If this little step is taken, then the human being also receives information other than sensory. In this moment it is possible that the mind (working until then only with sensations) was influenced by new information (coming via extra sensory perception). Such an influenced mind could have got back in balance with the soul and this would be the way to the own creation of reality, the path from slavery to freedom. This is what the gods could not allow to happen if they wanted to use human beings "as sheep".

That is why there has always been so much mystery around sex. There is "danger" (for the ones who control), that if the second chakra (gate) is activated, also the sixth gate is, and then the controlled human beings may liberate themselves from control. Sex was limited to reproduction. Experiences or potential work with energies released through sex became inconsistent with "pure faith". These words of the New Testament represent to me, the reaction to this restriction:

"A curse is on you, teachers of the law! for you have taken away the key of knowledge: you did not go in yourselves, and you got in the way of those who were going in."
Luke 11,52

In some spiritual friaries, sexual life was explicitly forbidden. It was described as inconsistent with the spiritual path. If an individual wanted to know more, become a part of the friary (system), he had to give up his sexual life. This is obvious nonsense that leads only to sexual frustration because sex is a natural need of the body. Nonetheless, most of the Christian clergy has the duty of celibacy, the absence of a sexual life.

If natural body needs are not satisfied, then the body is in imbalance with itself. What causes this imbalance, the soul? Not really. It is the mind, the part of the body which deviates the body from its own inner balance, imbalances – depreciates the body against the soul.

A different attitude is represented by so called "sacred prostitution", either as a church celebration of Eros (as a sexual god), or other "pagan" rituals or sexual practices from the period before and in the beginning of our calendar. This was, from the current point of view, "free" sex with more than one partner of both sexes. Pagans, some sects and also respected religions secretly abandoned themselves to those sexual practices.

From the original intention to use sexual energy for the opening of the sixth gate, it gradually became only an addiction to physical passion and there was often an unconscious agreement to be controlled by present (demonic) creatures.

Later, these rituals were declared to be dealing with the devil and cruelly combated. Together with ritual dances and communication with the elemental (present) creatures, this all was abandoned. In this way, men got rid of the natural access to the ability of extra sensory perception which they partly admired and partly envied of women.

All this was accelerated by the pope's declaration in 1484 which openly spoke about the possibility of sexual intercourse between demonic creatures and people. A few years later, the work "The Hammer of Witches" ("Malleus Maleficiarum"), was written. This work crowned the tendencies of oppressing women and rejected all extra sensory skills (which were most often described as black magic).

Similar behavior to women was not only a privilege of the Christian Church. Such behavior towards women of most cultures and religions had been formed (at unconscious level) hundreds of years earlier. In most ancient civilizations it was possible to kill women without any punishment, very often right after their birth, just for being female. Men were absolute rulers over women. Whether we look at the Chinese, Indian, Babylon or Assyrian civilization, Roman, Greek, Judaic, Christian and pre-Islamic civilization, females had the position of slaves. Compared to the above mentioned, the Egyptian civilization treated women the best.

We can find an exception in the treatment of women in one of the youngest religions – Islam, beginning with the teachings of the prophet Muhammad. Besides the current lack of awareness (fed by the present creatures of "Western civilization"), the position of women in Islam was the best which was possible to see. From the teachings of the prophet Muhammad, women in Islam had rights that women in the so called civilized world had fought for in the 19th and 20th centuries. See also the last words of the prophet Muhammad: "Be gracious to women!"

We have described how sexual life directly influences the abilities to perceive in an extra sensory way. Now, we will go back to the previously mentioned exchange of information between a man and a woman. A woman, in contrast to a man, has extra sensory perception naturally active. Women feel it all the time. This is what is called the female sense, female intuition, female perception or feelings. There are times when this perception is less intense or more intense, like around menses, during motherhood, etc.

Sometimes female reactions during these times are incomprehensible for men; incomprehensible because a woman reacts to a wider field of information than a man. Apart from sensory and rational reasons, a woman is also influenced by her extra sensory perception. In today's times, after hundreds of years, many women do not understand themselves anymore and fall under the male principle even in evaluating themselves and their behavior. The imbalance in a woman, her lack of confidence in what she feels, perceives and the effort to follow other (rational) reasons is the ground for problems in female areas, for example the ability to conceive, give birth, breastfeed and so on. A woman has her own "third eye" through which she can "see" more. A man does not have this "eye" naturally active, that is why he seeks a woman's presence. A man gains information thanks to connection with a woman. It is only a flash of information which he does not necessarily need to recognize rationally but he feels it as "satisfaction". A woman satisfies (saturates) the man's need for information. Therefore, women do not usually have such a need to change sexual partners as often as men. Women are able to perceive themselves. Besides the instinctual need of the body, there is one more reason why men change sexual partners so often. The reason is the exchange of information. Information is active in the areas of energy-information shells of the body and is mutually enriched during sexual experiences with a partner. During sexual intercourse of the physical bodies in the area of the second gate (genitals), many other "bodies", the coexisting energy-information bodies (shells), are connected.

Perception of this connection is not tangible. It remains in the form of feelings that can persist even for a very long time after sexual intercourse has taken place. Through sexual intercourse you transfer your information (feelings) to the other person, to his information field and at the same time you receive information from him. You influence each other. So, if you had sex with a person who for example is afraid of everything, does not believe in himself and suffers from depression, it is very likely that you will have the same feelings. Then, it depends on your level of consciousness if your feelings will transfer into emotions and start to poison you or not. In the chapter of creation of reality you will see how important these processes are and how they influence your life situation, your reality.

The exchange of information during intercourse always happens mutually with both partners. Birth control – either hormonal or physical – will not protect you from the above mentioned exchange of information and therefore, the choice of a sexual partner is always very important. Women understand this intuitively better than men.

For men, I will add the following. Be aware that information from a woman which will "stick" to you is not only her own information and feelings, which she carries and experiences deeply inside. She often does not even recognize this information herself or admit it. The kind of information which you get from a woman in this way, comes from her own (preceding) sexual life and her sexual partners. Simply said, through sexual intercourse with a woman you "download" fears and limits of another man who had a sexual relationship (e.g. even only one intercourse) before you. The woman does not need to be influenced by such kind of information because it is of the male frequency.

The same applies vice versa for information which a woman receives from a man. This information can be mixed feelings and limits of other women. A woman feels it intuitively and knows if her partner had been with another woman (if he was "unfaithful" to her). She senses another woman from him, something that has remained in him, something like a scent, some kind of addition (not a perfume). In fact, it is a frequency that another woman left in your partner.

The time for which you hold the foreign frequency varies from several minutes to months and its duration depends on many factors. It especially depends on the level of consciousness at which you are at the moment.

Be aware of the fact that each of your steps will be influenced by such "uninvited" frequencies. This is what it is about. Each of your decisions will have the flavor of such frequencies. Again, it is a certain lack of freedom.

In the chapter in which we dealt with the feet and walking, we explained questions like "Who are you going out with?", now we will explain the meaning of the question "Who are you sleeping with?" There is a direct connection because we are asking about what influences your behavior, decision making, in fact the creation of your own reality, right now. You already understand that your sexual behavior (who you have sex with) directly influences some of your inner processes. You can "stick" onto yourselves frequencies which will influence you and disturb you in your further life (in creation). This is the sexual subtext of the question: "Who are you sleeping with now?" Another subtext is in sleeping (with someone) itself. Sleep is still a great unveiled part of people's lives which has a substantial influence on the creation of reality. The following process is as "complex" as anything that we discuss from the transformation of consciousness point of view. In fact, the whole transformation is only a half part of the day. The same part is at night. Do you understand how complex issue we could have opened? Therefore, we will deal with this issue here just very briefly.

Our soul (own being) can, in the moments of sleep, leave our body and travel through existence to different places outside our reality. This is similar to what happens during the development of an embryo in the mother's body. The situation is even more complicated there, because the mind is not sufficiently developed yet and does not let the body (its intangible part) travel together with soul. Therefore, the body of an embryo changes physically – it goes through the development of all life forms on this planet, physically in part. This is enabled by an intangible part of a tangible body from which the mind is created later on and the mind will not allow this so simply. That is why days and nights are created for day and night activities; the activities of the body for – the male principle and for the activities of the soul – the female principle. If the mind sleeps, the soul can travel. This travelling soul projects in the form of dreams through certain parts of the brain to your own mind. Then you remember dreams. Dreams, your night reality, are a gate to another dimension. What you experience during the day is, from the point of view of a dream, unreal in the same way as a dream is from the point of view of an unconscious mind. It is too early to speak about it now. Looking from the basic phase of consciousness which I describe in this book, dreams can become a potential "training" area for your experiments to create your own reality. The phases of falling asleep and awakening are essential. The gate of dimensions opens and closes during these phases. You may have experienced a forceful "jerking" which felt like you were falling and this "woke you up" from the process of falling asleep. So far, only the soul can go through the gate. Before you fall asleep, deal with yourself, dream about how your life is changing. Imagine yourself living the way you would want. Visit personally (like your own being) the places in existence which contain the reality you would want to live in. Dreams have a direct influence on reality. It is so direct that it is necessary to get to a certain level of consciousness before you start dealing with this area fully. Dreaming is so powerful that it can even have destructive consequences in the beginning. Practice only conscious dreaming for now, try before each dreaming to "set" what the dreaming will be about. Maybe you already engage in this, although only for some aspects of life. If you dream already, try not to be only "an observer" but participate consciously in the actions which you experience "there".

If you master your actions consciously, you will realize that the skills which I have mentioned in this book work "there" more easily than in this reality (in the beginning).

There is power hidden in dreams but we will not uncover it yet. Its power is the same as the power of conscious creation. You will recognize it in the following way. Before each time you are falling asleep, remember the fact that you are trying to dream consciously. Suddenly, you will realize that the period between each falling asleep, when you realize this (in fact, all day!) is extremely short. Actually, you are still "only" falling asleep, as if your life starts to shrink when falling asleep. I will not uncover more at the moment. Soon you will realize why.

Part Two

The Creation of Reality

The freedom which you reach by realizing who you are and the principles described in this book, for example, can be used for the creation of reality which is around you. To make this happen, it is necessary to be in a certain phase of consciousness. An entirely unconscious person cannot do anything which I will briefly describe further.

Everything that happens around you is a result of creation. There are many creatures which have the possibility to influence things. But only human beings, like you, can truly create.

The principle of the creation of reality is one of the oldest principles in this reality. It is described in the Bible but also in other books dealing with spiritual growth or hermetic science. It is a phenomenon, which is easy to describe but not so easy, as you will soon recognize, to realize in practice.

In the Bible, this "art" is attributed only to God or to some acts of his "son" Jesus, or to the apostles in a limited way. It is about the ability to change reality, to change the real state of things. The Bible calls these acts miracles. These are the acts that, at first sight, oppose the possibilities of this reality and so to say, the standard abilities of people. If you do not let yourself be bound by the rules, then these skills (to create reality) are accessible to all people, without any difference.

How to do it? This is an easy question and there is an easy answer. Apart from religion, magic was also acknowledged as having the ability to influence reality. The pillar of magic, the only area of scientific examination to which the ability to create reality was acknowledged, is the knowledge – recognition written (among other things) down in the Smaragdine Table: *"That which is below is like that which is above that which is above is like that which is below"*.

We have already mentioned this statement but you may not still know how to use it practically. The key to create reality is hidden in this statement. We will examine this issue in this part of the book in detail.

The division of "below" and "above" perceive now as "inside" and "outside". These are analogical connections like in the mystery of the cross. Divine principles blend together and complement each other. The inside and the outside concern of course, a human being because human beings have been given these skills.

It is like swimming. Not many of you can swim without learning it from someone who can already swim. But we can surely agree that everyone can learn how to swim. Some can do it earlier, others later, there will be differences in speed and quality, but in the end anyone can do it. What do you need for it? Above all, you need to **believe that it is possible**. Then you need to understand how to do it and the rest is just practice. It is exactly the same with influencing reality. It is enough if you believe, understand how to do it and then you need to try it out and practice. After a certain time or maybe immediately, you will see how it works. But beware of words, you already know their power. The statement "It's unbelievable!", although pronounced in euphoria, when you see the result of your work, can bring the whole process back to the beginning and the new process could be much more difficult...

Faith, Decision at the Level of the Own Being Yes!!

The first thing you need is to believe that it is possible. What does it mean to believe? It is the same with both faith and decision making. There are two kinds of faith and decision making. At the level of mind and at the level of own being. At the level of mind you decide and say for example: "I will stop smoking." But if this statement is not supported by a decision at the level of the own being, it will not be realized, so you will not stop smoking.

Let me comment on this particular case. The above mentioned statement: "I will stop smoking" is a very unconscious statement. It uses the power of the word unreasonably if you consider the taken intention, which is not to smoke. If you say: "I will stop smoking" you are speaking about the future. You are saying that you will stop sometime in the future which is not realizable. The future does not exist, now. The only moment during which you create, influence, change, is the present moment. What should be the statement like? "I do not smoke."

Deciding in the way that you have known until now, is a decision at the level of mind, often amended by the statement mentioned above in the example of smoking. It does not work.

The decision at the level of the own being is what enables us to create reality. We will be dealing with it. It is very complicated to explain, so your entire cooperation and perception will be needed.

The whole process works the way that you, as a human being, have a judgment of the mind and the own being (soul) in balance. In balance means that both the mind and soul pull together, it especially means that the mind does not doubt what the soul knows. The difference between the mind and the soul is that the mind is realized at the interface of the tangible and the intangible world but the soul is purely intangible. The soul perceives all the possibilities and all the options as equally presumable. The soul does not assign any importance or any meaning to them. The mind, in contradiction, deduces and makes potential alternatives on the basis of facts, logic and experience, where one alternative is always the most probable one. Surely, you understand that to have the mind agree with a possibility about which the soul has no doubt, but which is not very "ordinary" (for the mind's understanding), can be a problem in the beginning.

I will liken it to the text of the Bible where it is described how Jesus walked on Lake Genesareth.

...When the disciples saw him walking on the lake, they were terrified. "It's a ghost," they said, and cried out in fear. But Jesus immediately said to them: "Take courage! It is I. Don't be afraid." "Lord, if it's you," Peter replied, "tell me to come to you on the water."
"Come," he said.
Then Peter got down out of the boat, walked on the water and came toward Jesus. But when he saw the wind, he

was afraid and, beginning to sink, cried out,
"Lord, save me!"
Immediately Jesus reached out his hand and caught him.
"You of little faith," he said, "why did you doubt?"
Mat 14,26

As you can see in the text, not only Jesus walked on the surface of the lake. When Peter was "charmed", he did not doubt the possibility of walking on the water and was able to do it himself. In the moment when the mind was activated, doubts came and Peter sunk and started to drown.

How is this possible? The mind, as we said, is influenced by present creatures. What the mind takes as reality, this is what it transfers to the body. We met with this issue in the first part of this book. Beware that without mastering of what we have already described, or at least a part of it, your further practice will be much more difficult.

If the mind was in unity (in harmony, in balance...) with the own being (soul), then it had no doubts. It said to the body: "It is ok. To walk on water is possible. I can see it myself! It is possible." The mind is supported by senses – which saw Jesus to walk (see also the meeting of Thomas with Jesus). In this moment, the mind was in unity with the soul. But in the moment when Peter realized that there is wind and recalled what wind does with a boat on water, his mind immediately started to calculate and imagine further possible (probable) developments of the situation. Disharmony with the soul occurred, which had not doubted, because it knew that it was possible (without even seeing Jesus). This disharmony caused Peter to be "disconnected" from the creation of his own

189

reality, and pulled him back to slavery, to the possibility of being influenced by present creatures (which brings a loss of the ability to create reality). This was Jesus's pronouncement: *"You of little faith," he said, "why did you doubt?"* It means that if Peter had not started to doubt, he could have – as Jesus – created:

One day he got into a boat with his disciples, and he said to them: "Let us go across to the other side of the lake." So they set out, and as they sailed he fell asleep. And a windstorm came down on the lake, and they were filling with water and were in danger. And they went and woke him, saying: "Master, Master, we are perishing!" And he awoke and rebuked the wind and the raging waves, and they ceased, and there was a calm. He said to them: "Where is your faith?" And they were afraid, and they marveled, saying to one another: "Who then is this, that he commands even winds and water, and they obey him?"
Luke 8,22

Let's overlook a religious (later added) value of this picture from the Bible and focus on Jesus' question: "Where is your faith?" It is the same faith as in the preceding example. Faith is a matter of the mind; the mind believes or not, doubts, needs proof. We can say that **the most spiritual** (the most intangible) aspect **of the mind is faith and the most material**, the least spiritual (the most tangible) **aspect of the mind is the instinct of self-preservation**.

There is a key question then. Why is it necessary to bring the mind (the representative of the physical body) to a more spiritual level at the creation of reality? In this way, we are getting to the beginning, to the statement from the Smaragdine Table. We have said that what is below = inside, is the same as what is above = outside. In other words, what is intangible is the same as what is tangible. Another description – what I feel inside, in my innate world, in intangible reality, is what I feel outside in tangible (material) reality. Is it clearer now? The way you perceive the world (reality), the way you perceive and "translate" it into your own "language" of good and bad is that what you perceive inside yourself. Then, the fact that you perceive some situation as "bad" for you will make it so that it will really be bad for you – and vice versa. Your perception, you, will trigger the way in which a certain situation will be realized in your reality. Yes, we are getting back to direct contact with Existence and its principles. You can now perceive the whole truth. The principle of creating reality is about your ability to realize your inner image of reality in the outside world. As, in the same way, you bring the outside material (real) picture into your inner world. So easy is the answer to the question which is in the beginning of the next chapter.

The Need for Freedom

What influences your ability to create reality? As I have already said, it is necessary to be free, at least in part. Partly free means to be aware of methods or ways which can take freedom away from you. We have dealt with this issue in the first part of this book. It is not necessary to practice all the described skills perfectly. The power of presence and of other divine principles lies in the fact that they function immediately, as soon as you use them; either consciously or unconsciously. We are of course most interested in using them consciously. You do not need to be a fully conscious being all the time in order to be able to create reality. You can, but you do not have to.

This is unconditional acceptance, but by whom? By God, Existence or whatever you like to call it. This reality has stepped into a new space. **Now you find yourself in the space of unconditional acceptance where you can realize yourself with plenitude.** If you create, then you are present with all that belongs to this state. From this, it is logical that if you are not present, you are not creating. However, the truth is that you create constantly but sometimes unconsciously, because presence is constant. In fact, there is only presence, nothing else. It is erroneous to think that you are not (cannot be) present. You can only be unconsciously present but you cannot be absent. It is only about realizing your presence. What prevents you from doing so? Present creatures do – see the first part of this book.

If you start dealing with how to be consciously present, everything is in fact done. Nobody is more present (a great mystic or a spiritual leader) or less present than someone else. We all are present in the same way. It is only about how often, or more exactly said, at how many places you are consciously present. In the moment when you are consciously present, you are equal with the beings which dwell consciously in presence in more than one place. It is not true that there are the holy and the holier. There are only two states – consciousness and un-consciousness. If you are the light, even for one second, from the successive time point of view, then you are a god. The same god who others adore in their unconsciousness for their whole life!

Yes, there are beings that dwell only in presence. To be more precise, beings that move consciously around all places of existence their reality. You may feel present only from time to time. You can consciously create reality in such moments. Do others have more of such places? Do not worry about that, deal with yourself. Nobody can create your reality for you. They can only control your mind because they wish you to create unconsciously = to let others create your reality. This is the substance of the statement. "You deal with many things, but there is only one which really matters." It is only up to you how you create reality for yourself.

If you deal with yourself according to the first part of this book, you will obtain the ability how not to lose (get back) your freedom, and this is a necessary presumption for further work, for obtaining (recognizing) the ability to create reality. One thing is not a condition for the other but if you master one thing, the other one will be much easier for you.

It is probably clear to you that if faith is the aspect of the mind and the mind would be controlled by present creatures, then it can be difficult. That is why, I recommend that you deal first with yourself and in the moment you start perceiving presence, maybe only for a little moment, then try to experiment with the creation of reality. In practice, both these areas are of course completely interwoven and it is possible to say that they are the same.

How to obtain the mind's faith? We will be dealing with this further. We have said that the essential state, in which you create, is presence. The presence in itself sets out harmony and unity of all parts of the trinitarian human being. If this reality is split into intangible and tangible parts, then the own being (soul) and the material body represent your realization here, on the planet. The third substance, spirit, is contained in both these parts; this is a kind of "food" of both the own being and the body. It is obvious that the tangible and the intangible are interwoven. That is why it is not possible to define purely intangible or purely tangible areas. These areas do interweave and influence each other directly. In fact, these are vibrations (frequencies) in the way we know them from physics, for example, the transmission of a TV signal. At the place where you are at the moment, there are many vibrations and frequencies all at the same time, for example a TV signal, a radio signal, the signal of a mobile phone operator etc. If you need to be convinced, you can switch on the TV, radio and make a phone call – all at the same time. TVs, radios or mobile phones are like "senses" which translate these vibrations to your body senses (sight, hearing etc.) and these senses translate them to the mind.

The senses enable the mind to perceive what it would otherwise not be able to sense, the senses intermediate a picture of reality to the mind. The mind plays a key role both in the sensation of reality and the creation of reality. The mind is, considering its position, very similar to the human being. **The mind is at the boundary of intangible and tangible, in reality similar to an individual who is at the boundary of what is realized and what is not (yet) realized in existence.**

The mind, physically realized in the brain which is the material organ of the human body, is a microcosm,

194

an image of something much bigger – macrocosm. The mind in the inside is what Space is in the outside. You can find it minimized along the same principles as in cosmos where they are maximized. Proportions are confusing here and directly correlate with a certain point of view. We are now interested in the principles and in understanding them. If the mind is in unity (will agree) with your soul, then it will picture, create, transmit to reality, realize and materialize images from your soul. It will make intangible frequencies tangible; to materialize the intangible. Then also space (cosmos), which is the mind, brain or the picture of the universe and existence, will realize the frequencies of your own mind. Let me now use inaccurate terms for even simpler (purposeful) clarification. Simply said, your imagination or images which you have inside (in your soul) will realize, materialize in reality. Of course, just as the "good ones", the images that you are doing well, as well as the "bad ones", which contain fears that something will not happen. What is inside is, in fact, the same as what is outside...

It is neither a miracle nor magic. You do not have to call it like that. In fact, it happens all the time, because you are also present all the time. You create reality all the time, not only if you consciously control the described ability. You also are present all the time, not only when you are fully aware of it. It is only about being consciously present and creating. There is nothing new that you will obtain, you have already had it for a long lime and you have also been doing it for a long time.

The own being, you, if you wish – the soul, is not influenced by reality like the mind is. The soul is aware, it is not necessary to convince it. The soul is connected with ego similarly like the mind with the material body. Both the mind and ego create a crossing between the spheres of the soul and body. Ego in its pure form is a necessary part because it has influence on the mind which then influences the body. In other words, ego is the moving force of intangible frequencies which are transformed to tangible ones through the mind and realize (create) via the physical body.

A simple example is of a carpenter working with a piece of wood. One of his hands is holding a chisel and the other one a hammer. The carpenter cuts a piece of wood and splinters of wood start to fly around. The carpenter is holding a knife and carving, Step by step you can see a certain shape arising from the unmade wood. What power is it which caused this to happen? Surely, we cannot say that it was the knife, chisel or the hammer which created it. All these tools took part but they were not the creating power. Were the hands of the carpenter the creating power? No, hands do not have this power, they were only mediators (like the knife, chisel and the hammer). Between whom and what were they mediators? Who really created it? Was it the carpenter? Who or what is the carpenter? Is he his body or his hand? Yes, he is in a certain sense but this is not the answer to the question we are looking for. The carpenter is a human being. Human beings are not only the body and soul, but also the spirit. The human hand, the human body was a co-creator, but only from one third. It was from the last third which had realized and cut the piece of wood. Are you starting to understand? Why did it happen and why did it happen exactly the way it happened? We will find the answer in other parts of the trinitarian human

Creation

196

*The mind is part of the body; not separate

being. Where does inspiration come from? From the own being, from you, from that who you are, from the soul. Inspiration, an impulse arises there. This impulse was, via ego, transferred to the mind and the mind used the body to create the result. The intangible frequency, at the level of the soul (own being), was via ego, the mind and the body transformed to a tangible one. In other words, an image of a wooden figure materialized. What was the real moving and life giving power which accompanied the whole process? Yes, the last third of the human being – the spirit is left. Spirit is the power that made the whole process real. Examine this statement thoroughly.

If you already know how to communicate with the body and soul, the last communication – with the spirit – remains. Spirit is a part both of the soul and the body and therefore, spirit is also an independent part. Acknowledging spirit is the highest knowledge. It has already been going on inside you because the spirit is the part of the body which you have been recognizing and also the part of the soul with which you have been communicating with. Communication with the spirit has in fact already been going on. This communication is completely natural.

The Body, Soul and Spirit

Spirit is a part of everything. Spirit is the power that puts creation into movement.

You are sitting and want to move your hand. However, the body in itself will not move it, the body is mass. You can object that I said that the spirit is a part of both the body and the soul, so why won't it move the hand? I also said that the body has its own intelligence which is able to intervene and move the body independently of the mind. Thanks to the body's intelligence, your heart beats without the mind's control, you wink if it is necessary, your hand will pull back "itself" if you touch a burning oven and similar. In these situations, the body decides itself and moves itself by power of spirit – in a certain sense it changes reality, but only to a very limited extent. The body is essentially controlled by the mind. The mind makes decisions. But even the mind in itself cannot control the body, create. If you want to move your hand, you can be decided in any way, but the hand will not move. Try it. Sit down and decide to move your hand. The decision at the level of the mind is not enough. The unity of the soul and the mind is necessary. It means that also the decision at the level of soul is necessary. The soul chooses from all the variants. The mind tells it which one to choose. If the mind comes to unity with the soul, the variant will be realized. How? By the power of spirit which can, thanks to the harmony of the own being and the soul, flow and become the creative power. At the moment when the mind and soul unite, the seal will click and the gate of spirit, which creates, will open. Try to perceive it and observe it. What is a part of your decision to move your hand from the point of view of the decision at the level of the mind and the decision at the level of soul and from the point of view of the own physical movement of the hand. Deal with understanding of this.

If the mind and soul find a common ground, the spirit is activated and by its presence the intangible frequency (image) from the soul will be realized to the tangible world.

This is the mystery of creating reality. There are more ways but the principle is one and the same. Harmony of the internal and the external; that what is inside is also outside.

How should we understand this in ordinary life? To describe it, we will use an opposite example, which you know well from your experience.

Circumstances, things that happen, often influence how you feel. In fact, what is outside is also what is inside (it becomes the inner or the inner becomes the same as the outer). We cannot change it. The outer and the inner are connected and therefore, it is not possible that an innately happy and satisfied person would experience lack, deprival or injury in tangible reality. In the same way that it is not possible for an innately unhappy and unsatisfied person to have a satisfying life. This can be changed and you have the power to change it – yourself. Everyone is god to himself, it is not given that you should live in suffering, that is nonsense. You should live to experience, to live out your life. In this way, through you, does God recognize Himself. That is why I wrote this book. I am showing how it is also possible to live, to understand and perceive reality; through the only possible way – through my own example. I cannot really give what I do not have myself.

Your mission in this reality is to live out, to experience, to recognize and to realize. Not to suffer or forbid yourself, to wait for something else to come along. There is neither heaven nor hell after life. There is only life and you are living either heaven or hell now. It is not necessary to suffer and think that you will be let to rest somewhere else at some other time. This is a kind of information manipulated by present creatures which control human beings as if they were sheep, most often through religion. Like Christianity which, although Jesus and others proclaimed a very deep truth, has been forcing people to live unnaturally under the threat of hell and with the vision of heaven – if they follow its rules. Where is the unconditional acceptance by God? Does it come only later, if you prove to be good? No, it is not there at all. Therefore, Christianity is an erroneous doctrine which is full of pain and fear. That is why we all have been embodied, in order to realize it here and now. There is no sense in waiting for something to come later on, there is no later on. There is only the endless now.

The question which remains is how to reach the state of oneness of the mind and soul. For this it is necessary to recognize the limits of any system. For example, the system of opposites (antitheses) – this is a very old system of knowledge describing reality and its principles. As such, it is applied to many spiritual and religious teachings. Therefore, it influences so many people.

Each system is limited. However limited by what? It is limited by itself and by the fact that it does not enable us to go further in our knowledge. The older the system is, the more impossible it is to extend it. A system at its creation continuously gives rise to a present creature which, in fact, is the system itself. A system – although it is immaterial – is in fact material because people, who believe in such a system, represent a material image (body) of a system. An immaterial part of the system is an entity – a present creature. This present creature is fed by the followers of a system. It is the same with the system of opposites which has originally come from true informa-

important understand and cliSest

tion about reality, but egos of its representatives, in fact their egoism, have spun this system round in the mind and sealed it. The truth is hidden even here – in the name itself. Antitheses (opposites) are not "positive" and "negative" or "good" and "bad" standing against each other. They are anti-theses, two equally existing, standing next to each other ideas, opinions. Not positive against negative. The dark disappears and the light stays. Neither of them needs to be either bad or good. That is why they do not really stand against each other but rather they "walk" side by side...

Why is it not possible to change the system? Because to do so, it is necessary to first go through the whole system, become its student, then an advanced master and then a great master. Then you can start changing the system. But a present creature will be of course trying to stop this. Just a few have succeeded in doing so and currently it is impossible. Present creatures which are in charge of the systems have their chosen ones. These people are preferred and given as an example to others. The newcomers are fascinated by the skills of the masters of a particular system. A director of a company can be such a master. The newcomer thinks that the director is the one who makes the decisions about everything. He has the power that enchants the newcomer. If he (the director) would want, he could do anything. This is really impressive and the newcomer voluntarily steps into the system, lets the system have his energy – he believes in the system (not in himself!). He is not aware that the director does not have power under his control. In fact, he cannot decide freely (he is just one part of a body). If he would do so and the system (a present creature) would evaluate such behavior as inappropriate for itself, the director would be "destroyed" immediately. He would be replaced with some other, more submissive director who believes more in the system than in himself. Such people are the chosen ones of the systems; they are the only ones who have some success, at least for a certain time. Everyone else only gives his or her freedom.

The system of opposites is a system which is **a curse of this reality.** It is superior to many other systems from which it gets energy. It is dogma which says that nothing exists without its opposite and that we can realize positives only thanks to negatives. When said like this, you do not yet realize the depth of this statement. We will use some examples to explain it.

If you are under this curse, then it is perfectly natural for you that there are "good" and "bad" moments in your life. You do not doubt this for a single moment. Most people believe and do not doubt that there cannot be only good all the time. The curse lies there. People believe that sometimes they are up and sometimes down; that there cannot be light without dark. No work, no money. Money does not grow on trees. This thought, this dogma, this curse is deeply rooted in many different situations. And this is the brake that prevents us from spreading our wings.

This dogma, the fact that people simply believe in it, that it is not possible – disallows many people to live fully. This has been entrenched in them since childhood. No wonder that if things have been going well for the past while, immediately the thought, "Watch out, it is coming, things will turn bad because the good things have already been" comes to mind. In fact, you cause things yourself by doing that. But why should it change? We do not doubt the existence of opposites now. Why is life, human beings or even God, forced to be pushed through this "pattern"?

There is neither "good" nor "bad". Equally, there are no coincidences. **Coincidences simply do not exist.** Only the mind perceives a certain situation being a coincidence because it cannot, from its experience identify a causal connection. This means that it cannot identify a cause to which the given situation would have been a consequence of. I said that antithesis is a curse that influences the perception of people in a certain way, as well as **causality is the curse of this reality.** It is not true that everything has its cause and its consequence. Situations are judged in this way by the mind. On the basis of the mind's understanding, both the systems of antithesis and causality (cause and consequence) were made up.

Many times you may get to a situation, when making a decision, when you ask yourself what is good. You think most of all about the consequences of such decision making (about a causal connection).

The answer is: nothing is good and nothing is wrong. Not everything needs to have its cause. **Presence withdraws itself from causal connections because a cause leads from the past to a consequence in the future.** There are simply various (non causal) options. It is the same with antitheses in presence. **There are no antitheses in presence because we compare good and bad to what happened (in the past) to what will happen out of that (in the future).** Many events are either good or bad depending from which point of view you are looking at them. For example, if you had missed a bus that had later crashed, then what was originally considered as bad, was actually good. There are many such examples.

You will be meeting these dogmas in yourselves when creating reality. The mind will constantly be offering you plenty of "unambiguous" scenarios of what would happen "if".

This is a very complex issue. The central point, which will show us the way, is again the middle of the cross, presence. Good or bad are in fact, directly connected with a consequence which will come. When? It will come in the future, obviously. **In presence there is neither cause nor consequence, neither good nor bad.** In presence, there is infinity and life, not limited, not bound by anything. This is not understandable for the egoistic mind. Why not? Because as I have said in previous chapters, the mind feels that it is mortal. The fear of death leads the mind to thinking over and over. Therefore, it sometimes tries, even fanatically, to examine and prove its truths (to whom? to itself, above all!). It is the same as people who are under its reign, under the reign of the mind. With the mind it is the same as with a limousine driver. He drives the limousine and decides himself during the journey where to go. This is allowed by its master (soul). The final destination is first known only to the master (soul). There are many ways and the driver participates in the choice. He only takes part, does not make the decision because he (the driver) does not know why he should go there. In reality, he is not the one who makes the decision about how and where to go. The one (the master) who is sitting in the back decides. But if the driver takes control and starts to follow only his decisions, it is very different for the one who is sitting in the back, he starts to lose control. The mind is not a servant any longer and starts behaving like a master. Watch out, the positions have not changed. The

over-analyzing

driver is still only a driver and the master is still a master. The problem is that there is the driver behind the steering wheel of the limousine (the body) and the master does not know how to drive. The driver becomes "the master" and the master becomes a hostage. The driver is not going to where he was supposed to; he drives according to what he thinks. An inner battle (inside the limousine, metaphorically said) between the driver and the master takes place. It is the same in the human body where the driver is the mind and the master is the own being (soul). Only if these two agree, the path (through life) can be perfect. Any disagreements lead only to disharmony. These are in fact illnesses, injuries and so on. Most often, the driver is stronger than his master and overrides his master. But it is a journey to the unknown for the whole crew because the driver does not know, only assumes, thinks and makes deductions. The master knows but he cannot do anything. He can only convince the driver to stop doing what he is doing. The driver is the mind, therefore he needs reasonable proof. It would be sufficient to let him drive through life and crash a few times and then say: "you see, listen to me, I knew where we were supposed to be going." The mind would certainly do it. But this comparison works only during childhood when a human being is still not under the control of present creatures. These present creatures give the mind a false certainty of the right choices.

In the example with the limousine it may look like the following. Consider a certain purpose and naivety of the story.

There is a politician and his faithful driver. There is also an opponent of the politician who wants to kill him. Both the opponent and the politician are publicly known, so they cannot come close to each other. The security measures of the politician do not enable this. Then a driver is hired to take the politician outside of all the security measures. The opponent hires a mediator who addresses the driver with an offer. The driver is told that the politician is critically ill and that they are doctors who have a miracle drug that will cure the politician. The driver says to himself that if the politician dies he will lose his job (will die with him). The driver wants to serve his master above all else and decides to help the master. He believes that there is no other way. He takes the problem into his own hands. He agrees to the set plan.

The driver's task is to bring the master to a certain place, to some underground garage where the opponent will be waiting. The driver is convinced that he is doing the right thing for his master. In the driver's opinion the master wrongly thinks that the driver is controlled and manipulated. The master does not really know how things work in everyday life (in this reality – the tangible). He is always sitting in his office (the intangible world unknown to the mind) and is not in direct contact with the surrounding world. Maybe he does not even know that he is seriously ill.

The opponent, aware of the politicians' abilities, just to make sure, follows the limousine on a motorbike, in case the politician convinces his driver, or if an accident were to happen.

The driver has an argument with the politician on the way, they may even fight and the driver loses control of the limousine from time to time, he can even damage the limousine a bit, but in the end they will get to the agreed place. The first thing that happens when the opponent approaches the politician is that he shoots the driver. Otherwise, the politician could escape if the driver would realize his mistake and drive away.

Now let us look at this story from our point of view like at a human being. The driver is the mind and the limousine is the human body. The master (politician) is the own being that inhabits the body (the soul if you wish). The opponent of the politician is some powerful present creature which is interested in the politician, in his soul. The one who played the role of the mediator, who convinced the mind, is also a present creature that represents for example some spiritual teaching, religious movement or egoism. The shielded limousine is the body, impregnable from the outside, perfect. It is possible to destroy the limousine by either crashing heavily (a fatal injury) or if you somehow get inside. There needs to be a slot created, through which it would be possible to get inside. It is clear that nobody is interested in the limousine because it is not about the body. What matters is the soul, the own being, the one who knows and is connected to the "government" (the politician), to God (soul). You either destroy him in the way that you destroy the body (the limousine) from the outside, a crash, a bomb or anything else, or you get inside. You need to open the door to get closer to the politician in order to use him for yourself. If it is not possible to influence him from the outside, then you need to get inside, set off an incapacitating (poisoned) gas and by doing so control the politician. To get inside the limousine (the body) is only possible if you create disharmony between the mind and the own being (between the driver and the politician). The politician cannot be influenced because he has all the information and can see through it. The only remaining possibility is to influence the driver (the mind).

Realize here, please, the following connection which may be shocking for some of you. If the limousine is the body, then the poisoned gas is a virus, infection or illness, generally speaking. You know that the limousine is armored and it is not possible to get inside; in the same way that the body is perfect and healthy. You have to open the door of the limousine. The politician will not open it, he is not foolish. The driver will do so. With the body, it is the mind which believes that it is possible. It believes that it is possible to open the door and let someone in. The mind started to believe in it a long time ago, in childhood, when your mother (who you trusted boundlessly) told you that you can get a cold from your sick friend or jaundice from unwashed hands and other things. This absolutely erroneous myth supported by one of the most powerful present creatures – medicine – is implanted in human beings from the early beginning. It is supported by the Old Testament god of Moses – "Ashes to ashes, dust to dust."

Already during pregnancy the mother goes to see a doctor who decides what is right and what is not. Later, the doctor examines the baby's development, whether it is progressing correctly or not. The baby is forced to be vaccinated. Into a perfect body, which a disease could otherwise not get into, illness is inserted through an injection. The body is in shock, it has not expected such a thing to happen. The same as the politician did not expect that somebody would open the door of his limousine from the inside and would let the poisoned gas come in. The body starts to create antibodies. This is the proof to the doctor's mind that this method works, that vaccination is a good thing. The mind will support it by the statistics of children who have survived only because they were vaccinated. This, and many more doctrines refined by the mind, kills human beings from the inside!

They influence your mind from childhood. All these who are controlled by present creatures. Beware of advertisements. Especially on the TV where images and sounds affect you together, which means more effectively. I am not talking about advertisements about washing powders. It is about the advertisements where serious people talk about the human body, about health and what influences it. The lesser evil is when they tell you that your joints will not be painful if you take their pills. These may even work for a limited time. The problem is when they use perfect computer animation and show you how the virus entered the body through the skin! This is a real threat. Your mind may accept this model because it will understand and believe in it. Animations are perfect and supported by medicine; and you are trapped. You have opened the door of your limousine and anyone can come in and influence you (the politician sitting inside). There lies the biggest danger. In inconspicuous affirmations, animations through which present creature codes you so that you are controllable. In fact they try to convince your driver – your mind, to open the door from the inside; or to take you somewhere, to crash your body and so on.

What do such assimilations mean? A crash, an accident is in fact an injury to the body. It is not true that you fell off your bike because of a coincidence or because you had just learned how to ride. This is in fact the outcome of a disagreement between the driver and the master when the driver sinks so deeply into the argument that he loses control of the limousine for a moment and crashes. It is either only a graze or a bruise or, sometimes it may be a broken bone. In diagnostics (of the transformation of consciousness) it is then easy to judge what (who) is behind this, where was the mistake. In a big accident the car can be destroyed and the body can be killed. If the driver (the mind) opens the door, if he believes the advertisement about the flu or to what "serious" people (doctors for example) say, then he allows a bomb to be thrown into the limousine. The mind allows infection to come into the body. It would not be possible otherwise!

What is disease in fact? It is the disharmony of the mind and the own being which is manifested by the body externally, most often as skin problems, eczema or problems connected with breathing. Today, many doctors have started to distance themselves from the control of the present creature – medicine – and have added other information and possibilities to their "repertoire" of diagnostics. It is not a coincidence that health is the most lucrative article in business. Pharmaceutical companies are very powerful and rich. Those companies have become more powerful than religion, as the mind has gradually been losing faith and fear has become stronger (instinct of self-preservation). Why is it like that? Primarily, it is about souls, to control them it is first necessary to be in cooperation with the mind – it is about opening the door of the limousine and getting into the body. We have said that the most intangible aspect of the mind is faith (the most compatible). Religious systems have worked with this principle. These systems have seeded fear which they use as a threat. Medicine has arisen out of the fear of death, to make life longer, to postpone death. All this is under the dictate of the male principle which is the fear creating division from oneness, unity.

On this basis, parasitic business sectors have been created. For example, insurance companies prey on peoples' fear. People get insured – what if... In this way they are making it obvious that they do not control their own lives, their path. They are under the control of present creatures. They may say that they are under the influence of events (as anyone else is) which they cannot influence themselves. That is not true. They just do not control their reality. They are not the masters of their limousine. They are drifted by so many events that very often they cannot get off this imaginary train themselves. It is going too fast. What else is insurance other than a manifestation of fear of what may come? This means that people show they cannot control their lives, their reality and need something or somebody who will help them out. **Where there is fear, there is no faith**. If fear (of the future) overrides faith (in presence), the mind loses the possibility to be in unity with the own being. The human being will lose the ability to create reality. More precisely said, human beings will hand this ability over to present creatures. Who would be interested in you being afraid? It is the one who wants to control you. We have dealt with this issue in the first part of this book, we have unveiled that what I am writing here has been really happening to you. If you, only once, perceive that it may be like this, you have won. Then you have brought faith to the mind and it will grow and strengthen along with other proof. The scales of faith and fear will start moving. How fast this movement will be and where the scale will get to, depends only on you. If you succeed to get a part of your freedom back, in fact you get your freedom back time to time for a limited period, then again you will speed up your awakening and you will start playing with the creation of reality. It is enough if you allow it and in the beginning, at least for a while, forget about rules and coincidences.

All of a sudden, the world around you will have new colors. Everything will be different, but still the same, only it may have brighter colors and you may sometimes feel a little dizzy. As if you had cleaned the front window of your car. Each breath will be different than before. Actually, nothing will change. Only your perception will change. This is the transformation of consciousness.

Let's go back to the issue of how to reach unity of the mind and the own being which is necessary for the creation of your own reality. I have shown in the above mentioned example how disharmony between the mind and soul can look like.

The truth is such that the mind is far more powerful than in the above-mentioned example. Realize that your mind can even kill you if you allow it to control your reality. It will not do such a thing because it is "bad" or "evil". It is perfectly natural for the mind to control the body and it has been doing so according to its best faith (which may be fear). And this is what it is all about, about faith. We have already mentioned it before and now we will continue. Faith is the most significant element influencing the mind, the same as fear.

If you are afraid, you do not have faith and if you have faith, you are not afraid. But in the beginning it is not so delineated, it is interwoven. We could say that the more faith you have, the less fear may influence you.

In the Bible, the significance of faith is mentioned in several places. Probably, the most apt is this:

"Don't be afraid; just believe."
Mar, 5,37

You can point out to a religious overtone, and why not? Faith is part of the mind the same as fear is. Both of them influence your decision making. Faith is very similar to fear when influencing the mind. It is up to each of you what you give priority to. Fear is connected with certainty. People search for certainty because they are afraid. They are afraid because they do not have faith. Who is not afraid does not need to search for certainty because he already has it. **Certainty and fear cannot exist together.** Someone has certainty because he has faith. It is not so important what he believes in. Sooner or later he will reach the truth and knowledge because there is only one.

In the early phase of the transformation of consciousness it is necessary to believe, to turn to faith. What should you believe in? Believe in yourself, in the perfection of Existence, in God. Let the mind deal with what belongs to it. Let the mind earn money if you feel you need more than you have. Support the mind with courage. Courage is self-confidence. Self-confidence creates courage, significance, the weight of words, the weight of decision making and the weight of consciousness. Self-confidence – consciousness of yourself – that you are. Freedom of the mind will liberate the own being, this harmony, this freedom opens, creates infinite possibilities for creation.

This is not connected with intelligence. Intelligence is a part of the mind. Intelligence has nothing to do with consciousness. An intelligent person will only understand faster if you explain something to him. However, he is not able to apply a particular kind of information to his life any better because he is unconscious. Peoples' intelligence is not what matters; it only influences language and the means through which the truth will appear.

You need faith; faith in the fact that it is possible. That is enough. It is enough if you recognize that something can be different. Different from what is commonly expected, for example that "money grows on trees"; simply stated of course. In the New Testament passage, which is below, there is the same information. You will see it if you allow it and let go of a certain religious formulation.

"Therefore I tell you, do not worry about your life, what you will eat or drink; or about your body, what you will wear.

Is not life more important than food, and the body more important than clothes? Look at the birds of the air; they do not sow or reap or store away in barns, and yet your heavenly Father feeds them. Are you not much more valuable than they? Who of you by worrying can add a single hour to his life?

And why do you worry about clothes? See how the lilies of the field grow. They do not labor or spin. Yet I tell you that not even Solomon in all his splendor was dressed like one

of these. If that is how God clothes the grass of the field, which is here today and tomorrow is thrown into the fire, will he not much more clothe you, O you of little faith? So do not worry, saying, 'What shall we eat?' or 'What shall we drink?' or 'What shall we wear?' For the pagans run after all these things, and your heavenly Father knows that you need them. But seek first his kingdom and his righteousness, and all these things will be given to you as well.
Therefore do not worry about tomorrow, for tomorrow will worry about itself. Each day has enough trouble of its own."
Mat 6,25

You are prompted not to take care of only the tangible part of reality. Do not let the mind, which only takes care of the body (mass), reign and worry only about food and clothing. Life is more than just food. Here the rebuke: "Faithless!" is used again. Let it be your relief on the path of the transformation of consciousness because even Jesus' followers had been searching only for their "faith".

If the mind (the representative of the body – the tangible part of reality) and the own being (the soul – the intangible part of reality) are in unity, you do not have to take care (be afraid) of food, drink and clothing (symbols of basic needs of the body). You do not have to because information about this need (food) is a part of unity because the mind is contained and knows what the body needs.

Searching for "the kingdom of God" and its justice is in fact finding the intangible part of reality; first of all the intangible substance of the human being which is the soul. If you find it (or at least if you accept its potential existence), the imaginary scale starts moving. And this leads to one thing – the retrieval of balance between the own being (soul) and the body (the mind which "represents" the body).

If you get to the a state which is at least close to balance, then various "coincidences" will start happening to you which will, as it were, solve your problems – expectations in life. This is that the rest of what the body needs (food, drink, clothing etc.) will be added to you incidentally.

When will this happen? It will happen if you are present. "Therefore, do not worry about tomorrow" – symbolizes the need of presence. For the interpretation of the quotation now you see that if the truth is contained in something, it will appear (in) itself. Light will go through the tiniest slit, the same as water which also carries information.

As many times before, I am reminding you again: practice everything that I have written about. Otherwise it will not work. Just for a while, try to believe that you deserve to have a great life without even having to work hard. That you do not have to go anywhere, you do not have to do anything else. Except that you start to believe. To believe that it is possible. You do not have to call it god. It is not about symbols or names. It is about one thing – only one thing matters, if you allow this to happen, if you start to believe that it is possible. It is enough, nothing else. You will receive signs sooner than you think. The only necessary thing is to have your eyes and ears open. You will see what "coincidences" will start happening to you.

" Deal with yourself "
(focus) (on)

Observe everything but do not judge anything. When the first sign comes you may overlook it but that does not matter. More of them will come. Observe yourself and as soon as you start smiling you will have won. You will be laughing in the beginning but do not say "It can't be possible" or other similar pseudo negations. As soon as you catch yourself smiling gently and imperceptibly at some situation – "some coincidence" – you will immediately feel contact with the original Being. In this moment, you will be aware of what has happened. This is the Mona Lisa smile. It is the conscious smile of someone who knows... Perhaps the more sensitive people in your surroundings will ask you what has happened. Do not explain, do not answer. Keep it to yourself. You yourself had been searching and you have found. Enjoy the contact with yourself. Your abilities will multiply. The next sign will seem much clearer, more obvious to you. You may even be looking around yourself. You may have the need to share it with someone. How is it possible that nobody else other than you can see it?! It is so obvious! Like this you will free yourself. The light of truth will emblaze a flame. You will become "the light". A small flame that someone can switch off in the beginning, therefore keep it (for now) only for yourself. Deal with yourself, you will be rewarded more than you expected.

Do not let yourself get confused by enslaved people, or become unhinged from your faith, maybe even the closest people will be trying to discourage you. Forgive them. ✶✶✶

"A prophet is honored everywhere except in his own hometown and among his own family."
Mat 13,57

But if you still have the persistent urge to tell people in your surroundings what has happened to you, then be aware that:

"You are the light of the world. A city on a hill cannot be hidden. Neither do people light a lamp and put it under a bowl. Instead they put it on its stand, and it gives light to everyone in the house."
Mat 5,14 Exposure to the "light" is enough. People will realize what they already know.

We will use the power of faith, which is the most spiritual (the most intangible) frequency of the mind, to reach harmony of the own being and the mind. We will believe that what is going on inside – in thoughts, in images – is possible to shift, to materialize and to realize also on the outside. This means, through our own ideas, to create a new different reality, the reality we want to have.

This is not fiction, this is reality. I know that the mind that has not yet encountered anything similar, will deny this information immediately. The mind needs proof.

As we have already stated, it has been happening in fact all the time, because you are present all the time. You cannot be absent, exist either in the past or in the future. It is not possible. You exist only in the presence. The difference is if it is conscious presence or not. Conscious presence is freedom. Unconscious presence is enslavement to the System. Similarly, it is not possible not to create your own reality. You create it all the time. You do it either consciously or unconsciously. Unconscious creation is the state when you are saying or thinking: "How is this possible? Why did this happen to me (again)? Why me?" This kind of statement proves absolutely unconscious creating. The system of opposites tells you that there is always a bit of evil in every good. It is not possible to be doing well all the time. Religion tells you that if you are not obedient, you will go to hell. Everything frightens you and controls you via the fear of something unreal – via fear of the future. If you are doing well at the moment, it doesn't mean that some kind of catastrophe will come. Be aware that you create that which happens around you. If you do not think over and over about a potential threat, it will not happen. Those are the people about whom you ask how is it that they are doing well all the time, it is not fair. Justice is another false conviction. It is connected with judgment and judgment is connected with good and bad. If there is no good and bad, there is no judgment, no justice. It does not mean subjection or injury, it means unconditionality and freedom. "Evil", a process named by the mind like this, serves to recognize "good", which is again a process the mind needs to give a name to. If you recognize good, then you do not have to experience bad. It is about realizing that "good", the state which you like and not to step out of this state. The System, for example the system of opposites, forces you to step out of it again. If you feel well, then it is only "thanks" to (or with help of) bad and because these two principles move, it is regular that bad must be followed by good. Nonsense! It is a construction of the mind and fear! Stop this curse, avoid the karma attachment. Open your arms and shout: "I am!" Nobody and nothing is standing in your way except for you...

Faith is the most intangible aspect of the mind. Gradually, you will learn to perceive within yourself the state when your faith is firm and when it is not. The path to firmer faith goes through practicing the principles described in the first part of this book. As soon as you realize which principles really work and function in this reality, using them will be then for you as simple as riding a bike. But if you do not start to practice, to live (out) these principles, then nothing that I have described here will be possible.

"Why do you call me, 'Lord, Lord,' and do not do what
I say? I will show you what he is like who comes to me
and hears my words and puts them into practice. He is
like a man building a house, who dug down deep and laid
the foundation on rock. When a flood came, the torrent
struck that house but could not shake it, because it was
well built.
But the one who hears my words and does not put them
into practice is like a man who built a house on the
ground without a foundation. The moment the torrent
struck that house, it collapsed and its destruction was
complete."
Luke 6,46

"Digging deep" is the path which everyone walks when dealing with themselves. It unveils many deeply stored fears and anxieties; unsatisfied needs from childhood (see the chapter about children) and many other "weights" which are carried on your own "cross". You will deal with them all. You will recognize and accept them. You will use the principle of light and the shadow will disappear. Shadow will change from misunderstanding to light (recognition), without a fight.

Through everyday practice, as you live with yourselves, you will be strengthening your faith in yourself and in the principles described for example in this book.

And he said to all,
"If anyone would come after me, let him deny himself
and take up his cross daily and follow me.
For whoever would save his life will lose it,
but whoever loses his life for my sake will save it."
Luk 9,23

How to understand this quotation?

"If anyone would come after me" – to the heavenly kingdom which is a satisfied state of freedom and wealth;
"let he deny himself" – your mind which feels to be you, will hold off and give arguments why not to do it, without even trying (you know this well, don't you?);
"take up his cross daily" – every day you will be approached by present creatures, you will be carrying your cross, your symbol of presence, you will be making decisions (cross) where to go in every single moment, you will be tempted;
"and follow me" – the power of now.
"For whoever would save his life will lose it;" – only the mind alone cannot save you, the mind itself does not create;
"but whoever loses his life for my sake will save it." – from the mind's point of view, you will lose life if you do not follow the mind (do not behave reasonably), but if you "lose" it for the moment of now, for presence, you save yourself.

221

Third Chakra - Solar Plexus
Stomach

It is important to recognize the mind as part of the human being. We have said that the mind is a certain entity, a creature that inhabits our physical body. The mind is an intangible entity realized at three places of the body; twice in the area of the head – the front (big) brain and the back (small) brain and once in the area of stomach – solar plexus. This is what we are now interested in. The area of the stomach is the area of the third gate (the third energy centre, the third chakra). This is very important. This is the point through which human beings are controlled by the present creatures. This area is the point where fear has settled. You certainly remember it for example, from school years, when you didn't feel well – in this area – when you were expecting a problem or were afraid of (what might come – of the future). Humans are controlled through fear. Fear, in its pure form, is the opposite of faith. That is why it is not possible to confuse these two terms.

But in the masterpiece presented by present creatures, in **the belief systems** (for example religions) this confusion is possible and faith is connected with fear into one huge power that controls human beings. This is the system of sugar and the whip, good and evil, the opposites. This reminds us of the beginning of this chapter, of the curse of the opposites.

Faith as part of the mind is placed in the area of the third gate. The solar plexus is then the centre of our power or weakness, the point through which energy comes in. The masters of martial arts know this and are particularly interested in this point of the human body. This point is then divided into smaller centers (more micro brains – "minds") but this is not important for us now. Solar plexus is a very important place. Metabolic processes take place here. From tangible to intangible energy (in biology, ATP is presented as the softest energy, but from our point of view, this kind of energy is still tangible). In this area the soul, the own being, appears. From the zodiac point of view, it is the area of Virgo's and Leo's actions. Virgo influences (from below) through the frequency of the mind (fear) and Leo (from the above) through the frequency of ego (faith, courage).

What is substantial is that we were unable to work with this centre actively. For the purpose of the above mentioned need (see the chapter about sex) to maintain human beings as manageable "sheep". The third gate is the gate where the creation of reality is manifested. It is the gate, the centre of the sun (solar plexus) where faith (fear) is placed, which will enable us (or disable = fear) to reach the balance between the internal and external (between the soul and the body) and to create our own reality. The third gate is the place where the tangible meets the intangible and harmony is created, so to speak, the conscious management of the course of life. With the involvement of both the lower (the first, the second chakras – the tangible) and the higher (the sixth, the seventh chakra – the intangible) gates, right here, the light or sun that shines through (creates) our life, our reality, is generated here. As I have mentioned before, this gate is connected with the fifth body gate and these gates are two halves of the third seal of the Holy Trinity, because the fact that you are able to create, directly influences your future. Through this gate, the mind is attacked by present creatures (and then emotions arise as described in the first part of the book). You can sense both tangibly – through sensory communication (the fifth chakra) and intangibly. You can feel it physically if the gate suddenly (a shock) or for longer period (a pressure, stress, fear) closes (a kind of pressure in the stomach), you can become lost for words, because of the connection of the third and the fifth chakra. For example stammering comes out of this. It is a deep-seated fear. The speech impediment that Moses had arose from this, from experiences which he had at Mount Sinai.

"At this, Moses hid his face, because he was afraid to look at God."
Exodus 3,6 (2nd Book of Mosses)
And he said: "Behold, I make a covenant: before all your people I will do marvels, such as have not been done in all the earth, nor in any nation and all the people among which you are shall see the work of the LORD for it is a terrible thing that I will do with you."
Exodus 34,10 (2nd Book of Mosses)

If you are very afraid, you spread it around you through this third gate and if you have deep faith, then you spread this faith as light. Why? Because faith – the intangible (the most spiritual) aspect of the mind – is an expression of harmony between the mind and the own being (soul). If you have faith, you are in harmony with your soul. In fact, your own being (you) is in harmony with your body, in oneness with the mind. Then everything will come true for you. It is enough to "have an idea" and it will happen. Your intentions will come true, everything will go well. Problems will be solved, so to speak, without any effort if you notice any at all. You create reality.

If you have faith, not fear, then miracles will happen (from the point of view of the frightened mind), in other words, you simply create your own reality, and you are using your divine inheritance.

And a woman was there who had been subject to bleeding for twelve years, but no one could heal her. She came up behind him and touched the edge of his cloak, and immediately her bleeding stopped.
"Who touched me?" Jesus asked.
When they all denied it, Peter said, "Master, the people are crowding and pressing against you."
But Jesus said, "Someone touched me; I know that power has gone out from me."
Then the woman, seeing that she could not go unnoticed, came trembling and fell at his feet. In the presence of all the people, she told why she had touched him and how she had been instantly healed. Then he said to her, "Daughter, your faith has healed you. Go in peace."
Luk 8,43

How is this possible? Because only this woman amongst the crowds that were so close to Jesus really believed (needed) that Jesus would save and heal her. Because she believed, it really happened to her. Jesus as a fully conscious being had even felt her touch.

How is faith connected with touch? This is interesting. Touch is a sensory perception (the fifth chakra – senses). The senses, as we have said, represent a kind of screen of (tangible) frequencies. Physical (body) aspect has only the mind, senses are connected with the mind (the body). Therefore, touch is the mind's sensation.

✳ If the woman needed to touch, her faith was not entire yet. She had no doubts but she needed energy of both the third and the fifth gates, so that she could create her future (recovery). This happened through touch. She believed (the third gate) and touched (the fifth gate), in this way she gained the key of the third seal of the Holy Trinity (see the third chapter of the book) and she influenced, created her future according to her intention which was to recover.

As I have said, it is enough to have an idea, a word is enough. More precisely said, to be fully aware of your own faith.

There a centurion's servant, whom his master valued highly, was sick and about to die. The centurion heard of Jesus and sent some elders of the Jews to him, asking him to come and heal his servant. When they came to Jesus, they pleaded earnestly with him, "This man deserves to have you do this, because he loves our nation and has built our synagogue." So Jesus went with them.
He was not far from the house when the centurion sent friends to say to him: "Lord, don't trouble yourself, for I do not deserve to have you come under my roof. That is why I did not even consider myself worthy to come to you. But say the word, and my servant will be healed. For I myself am a man under authority, with soldiers under me. I tell this one, 'Go,' and he goes; and that one, 'Come,' and he comes. I say to my servant, 'Do this,' and he does it."
When Jesus heard this, he was amazed at him, and turning to the crowd following him, he said, "I tell you, I have not found such great faith even in Israel." Then the men who had been sent returned to the house and found the servant well.
Luk 7,3

Only by words he did make miracles, without touch. His faith in himself was so strong that he spread his faith amongst others only by being present. Examine this statement (this sentence).

If you do not have faith, you only follow the mind and then you are more familiar with feelings of fear, you feel defeated. By what, maybe by life, by circumstances? You do not believe in yourself and the more someone makes this fact obvious, the more you are able to fight for your "honor". Because this is your weakness.

I will unveil one mystery to you. The real masters of martial arts (but also magicians) can "control" you even without physical contact. They can sense, see (the sixth chakra) weak points in the energy field of your physical body and they "touch" you slightly (intangibly) at certain places. I am sure you have experienced a situation when some news (a word), knocked you to the ground. Someone said something, maybe not even directly to you, and it broke you – inside, you may have even cried. Something touched you energetically. The situation we are describing is identical. It only depends on how you focus the energy which you want to use to influence someone. We will use an example that you surely know. If you are able to upset someone by saying a few words, it is the same as "secret masterful hits". It is not about any physical (motional) art, it is about working with energy.

I am mentioning this so that you can better understand how present creatures (or their embodied allies) can influence you.

I have said that an individual controlled by the mind, by fear, takes life as a battle. He has to overcome various obstacles all the time. Either, because he thinks that someone intentionally does not want him to do well (harms him purposely) or just because it is simply like that.

Such a person is without any courage inside him (see the definition of courage above), without any self-confidence and he tries to amend this lack through various "courageous" (adrenalin) activities. Or, if he does not feel like doing those activities, then at least some other activities which are "in" at the moment, typical for the time and place where he lives. He also tries to help and save others. Therefore, he has many "friends" who "need" him. This all has something in common – it is desire to gain the appreciation of others (to raise his significance). Such a person of course denies that he does that. He says that he does it because he is simply like that, not to get appreciation from others. That is not true. These are mostly very intelligent but also egoistical prisoners of their own bodies, life and reality. Such disharmony occurs most of the time in childhood (or in the period until the age of 21). You can even see it physically. Such people are usually either overweight or constrained. Those are two very close states (not at first sight) when a person is not successful in finding harmony with himself. The common denominator of this is fear. These people usually have problems with digestion, blood pressure, the liver and so on.

Let's get back to the topic. For the creation of reality, oneness of the internal and external, of the intangible and tangible, of the own being and the physical body and of the soul and mind is essential.

In the following quotation we can find a link to this oneness:

*"Again, I tell you that if two of you on earth agree about
anything you ask for, it will be done for you by my Father
in heaven."*
Mat 18,19

In other words, if oneness of the mind and soul occurs
– two of you (three) get into agreement and "ask", which
means they will realize how to create – it will happen.
As we have said before, the mind is a microcosm in relation to the space that surrounds us, which is in fact
a macrocosm. You can understand "Father" in the above
quotation as the macrocosm that surrounds us. Here
is the direct analogy or similarity with the quotation of
the Smaragdine Table; that which is below is that which
is above. That which you will be creating inside yourself
(secretly in the soul) will be realized in the outside (your
"wishes" will materialize in the real world).

Let me use a text which was not included by the
church into the New Testament. We can find a much
clearer explanation in the Gospel of Thomas in which is
written:

Jesus said to them: "When you make the two into one,
and when you make the inner like the outer and the outer
like the inner, and the upper like the lower, and when you
make male and female into a single one, so that the male
will not be male nor the female be female, when you make
eyes in place of an eye, a hand in place of a hand, a foot
in place of a foot, an image in place of an image, then you
will enter the kingdom."
Thomas 22

You can see that it does not matter which image of the truth you use, either the one from Jesus or from Hermes in the Smaragdine Table. The truth is the light and the light is the only one as the truth is the only one. Added religious amendments or manipulation is rational (material). They are shadows that the mind uses to obstruct the light (the truth).

We can find a similar message in the following quotation:

"And when you pray, do not be like the hypocrites, for they love to pray standing in the synagogues and on the street corners to be seen by men. I tell you the truth; they have received their reward in full. But when you pray, go into your room, close the door and pray to your Father, who is unseen. Then your Father, who sees what is done in secret, will reward you."
Mat 6,5

Understand the prayer here as dealing with yourselves, as reaching harmony, oneness of mind and the soul. A person discovering internally does not need to pretentiously show that he prays. The original sense of prayer (which is similar to meditation) is personal inner searching. Therefore, prayer is most of all a personal act. It is a personal dialogue (with God). Not a mass church event to which inner searching has gradually turned into.

In the following part it is more interesting, it talks about the Father (God) who we can understand for example as a macrocosm (space) in the way "your Father", not as a herd-like expression as "our Father". Let us continue: "your Father, who is unseen" – he is not tangible and sees (senses) intangibly (secretly for the mind). That is why this oneness at the intangible level is necessary. Further on: "he will reward you", which is tangible, material – a realized intention outspoken "secretly", intangibly. At the level of decision making by the own being (soul) with the support of the mind = oneness of the soul and body (of the own being and mind!).

As you can see, the information that I am bringing, is not new. It was not new even two thousand years ago. It is only necessary to realize it and that's it. I will repeat once more the following quotation:

"Therefore consider carefully how you listen. Whoever has will be given more; whoever does not have, even what he thinks he has will be taken from him."
Luk 8,18

In fact, who has faith, will be given the mind and who has no faith, will lose even that which the thinks the has – the will lose the mind which the had thought would save thim. This is the last stage when a person, simply said, becomes insane. The struggling of the soul is so enormous and unbearable that a person mentally collapses (thanks to the self-preservation instinct). Or he can attempt suicide. He cannot go on. This is the last calling for help and if someone undermines it, then the return is extremely difficult, if not impossible. Recognizable behavior usually precedes this state but the deaf and the blind will not notice it.

"Can a blind man lead a blind man? Will they not both fall into a pit?"
Luke 6,39

231

When such a person then gets under the control of medicine represented by psychiatrists and psychologists he is usually drugged up by various medications and considered "uninfluencable through treatment" case. Only faith can then be the last factor that can change a seemingly unchangeable situation because:

"For nothing is impossible with God."
Luke 1,37

What is this factor that can influence the unchangeable? It is this ability to create your own reality. The soul does not have a problem; it is open to all the options. It is necessary to convince the mind; the mind that started to believe that nothing more can be done. Of course, neither the doctors, parents, a psychologist, a teacher nor I myself, know what to do... If the mind can be convinced to accept, only for a single moment, more than one option, then light will appear. Light will start to come through this slot in the mind and enlighten anything it encounters.

That what erects the wall between your mind and you are in this case drugs. The more drugs someone uses, the less he can communicate (again you can see here the relationship between the third and the fifth body gate). This wall, which stands in the way of light, creates a shadow. The bigger the wall is, the greater the shadow. This shadow is created by obsessed beings – those who give out the drugs. Obsessed beings who are obsessed by shadows of the past with their willing to help – to do good; from the outside, using the male principle which separates. They do good deeds and influence others, but they themselves are not in harmony. They cannot give what they do not have themselves. The final states of "insanity" which you can see in psychiatric institutes have nothing in common with life. A person who went through treatment sits on or lies in bed and stares intently into nothingness, into the nothingness of his being. In many cases, the soul is not there anymore, it is "only" the physical form.

A long path leads to such a state and it is possible to step aside from it anytime. If you have particular information or enough faith (in yourself, in life).

Now we will again speak about the trinity of human beings. Humans as trinitarian beings contain three substances of equal significance, value, size or whatever you want to call it. These are the human body (the physical container), the own being (soul) and the spirit (divine power).

If we would compare a human with other beings inhabiting this reality, we would not find any other being having these three substances in complete balance (oneness). This equates a human with god (considering "genetic" equipment and skills). These three substances have (ideally) the same "size". It is not the same with other beings.

Now let us look at what this means practically. The degree of spirit determines the ability to create your own reality. The greater degree of spirit present in a particular being, the bigger the ability of this being to influence his reality. In nature that surrounds us, we can see it in predators. These are beasts or any animals that hunt other animals. These beings have a greater ability to create – to influence reality – than the beings which are hunted. From this point of view, the term intelligence has arisen and it is often wrongly confused with the degree of spirit. The lower the degree of spirit, the lower the "order of embodiment" (here you can see a certain analogy with some Eastern religious paths – India). But we are still dealing with animals that move. Movement, in fact, is the primary manifestation of spirit (life power). The higher the degree of spirit, the more difficult movement a being can make and the other way around.

Vice versa, if we lower the degree of spirit, we will get into the kingdom of plants. Plants also move and influence their own reality, but to a very limited extent. If you film a plant for a few days and then you play it during a few minutes, you can see how "lively" they are.

If you lower the degree of spirit to a minimum, then you will get into the realm of minerals. It is very relative to speak here about life because the degree of spirit is so low that we cannot watch the activity of minerals through our senses. But they are alive. Thanks to a certain degree of spirit, even minimal, that everything contains. The time period which would record their "movement" would be not of days but of hundreds of years during which rocks move and change.

As I have said, the three substances of human beings are blended altogether. They are contained one in the other. The human body is the tangible projection and at the same place the own being is the intangible projection. Both substances blend into one another. Where is the third substance – the spirit?

Spirit is contained in both substances at the same time. It is, so to speak, separated (from this the mind created duality, the system of opposites). However, this is not an exact description. The spirit is contained in the body and the spirit is also contained in the soul. Thanks to "viability" – the degree of spirit, beings such as the mind in the body and ego (a being in the soul) "come tolife". By the perfection of spirit, no changes, no motions would happen – although, or rightly because of this perfection, motion (life) occurs. The soul as a being knows, it is connected with God (with the essence, with the core) and does not need to change things. The same applies to the body. Spirit the Divine power bring the need to change and realize. Spirit contained in the body brings life to the body. The body is not only biochemistry; scientists discovered this fact a long time ago. What is there in addition, what the mind can never create? The substance of spirit which is not material at all (neither tangible, nor intangible), we could call it will but we would not get any closer to real clarification which is actually not possible.

The substance of spirit causes the creation and development of the mind, as an intangible being and as a body organ (the brain). Similarly, the own being is in fact a certain cluster of energy – an intangible entity existing on principles that we have not fully discovered yet. From a certain point of view, the soul is as "material" as the body is, but "materializes" on different frequencies. Not even the soul could "live" if not for the substance of spirit. This evokes the creation of the ego. The ego is something like an engine of motivation. It motivates us to follow inspiration. Here you can see that **both the mind and the ego are your allies**, literally. That they more likely put you into situations which are not favorable for you, is because you are not fully aware and you let them control you. More precisely said, **you let yourself be controlled through them by someone else** (by present creatures).

Yet, after receiving the above information, you can realize why a diminishing degree of spirit influences the ability to create reality.

Now we will be dealing with the other substance of the human being – the own being or the soul. How is it with the soul? Does its degree also diminish? Not quite. Let us say that it is necessary to understand this substance in a different way. It is clear with human beings, it is by virtue of the divine trinity. But how is it with animals and other beings?

Animals, plants and minerals also have their own beings but the number of bodies (the tangible "container"), which are connected with one own being, is different. We can use an analogy with the degree of spirit. The higher the degree of spirit, which is the ability to control reality, the less the bodies are parts of one own being. Simply said, for example a tiger has its own soul. On the contrary, an ant does not, but ants as a community have their own being. Here you can see that using a term soul would not be very convenient here. Therefore, I have been using both terms – the own being and the soul – in the text. The soul as a more established term and the own being as a more convenient term.

There are different degrees of spirit around us, some of them you can recognize immediately, some of them are hard to imagine. Does an atom realize itself as a part of a stone, as a part of a mountain, of the Earth, of the Milky Way? The same applies to a human if he stares upwards.

The number of "bodies" with minerals is proportional to the measure of space. That is why people in ancient times could worship a mountain for example. They were able to perceive it as an entity. The truth is that the mountain is something like an ant, "only" a part of "the body" which is the whole Earth.

Back to the creation of reality. We have said that the ability to create arises from the oneness of the mind and the own being. Unity, or harmony means that they are not in conflict, that they do not doubt. That is why it is necessary to convince the mind because the soul knows and does not doubt. How can we convince the mind? We have been doing it all the time and we will continue to do so.

It is possible to reach oneness of the mind and the own being only in the present. For this, it is necessary to keep the mind in the present. Information about how to do it is in the first part of this book. As I have stated, emotion is one of the factors why the physical body gets older. By emotions we poison the body which then gradually dies. At a certain point, it will die entirely. So, if you know what and how is emotion caused, you are then on the way to unity of the mind and the own being.

In the Old Testament, it is said that people before "the flood of the world" had lived much longer than afterwards. Age was counted in centuries. How is it possible? People had not been under the control of present creatures, which were only then just being created. The break point occurred after the flood of the world, or after what is described as this flood. As I said, people started to be controlled via mutation of DNA. People started to turn away from the presence more and more and their bodies started to age. Time has been gaining its "strength". Time has been counting down to death faster and faster.

It does not have to be like that. This mystery is hidden in the following quotation:

"Follow me, and let the dead bury their own dead."
Mat 8,22

If you look to the past all the time, you are already dead. Because you live that which no longer exists, what is already dead. Presence offers current life, without the dead (without the past). The deeper your faith is in the presence, the less controllable you are via emotions (the past, the future), and the less your body will be poisoned and be dying (ageing). Death is not a definite part of the presence.

"Some of the present standing here right now will not die before they see the Kingdom of God."
Luke 24,6

Those who are present will not taste death. This quotation is about two thousand years old. Another quotation is similar:

"Why do you seek the living among the dead?"
Luke 24,5

Why do you seek current life (the present) where it is not – in death, in the past? Which is a basic and widely spread paradox from the Christian symbol of the cross and Jesus Christ.

I have mentioned it before and we will get back to it here. The crucifixion of Jesus – as a symbol, is active when

Jesus touches the middle of the cross by the fourth gate of his body, where there is infinite life, the truth and love. This is the path. As he said:

"I am the way and the truth and the life."
John 14,6

This symbol, although it occurs in some church systems nowadays, is not so known. But the symbol of tortured Jesus, dead Jesus, is very well-known even among so-called atheists. This is the symbol of dead Jesus where his head rests in the middle of the cross (below).

We will stop at the crucifixion itself for a moment. Co-incidences do not exist and it is not a coincidence that the place where Jesus was crucified is called Golgota which, in translation, means the skull.

This symbolically corresponds with the placement of the mind in the human body. It was the Mind which crucified him. Not the mind as a part of his body (as of the human being), in this case, but the Mind as a super creature, we can call it the SYSTEM. This is something that we have not encountered jointly yet. And this crea-ture shows such a symbol – dead Jesus – as its triumph. The Mind took over control of faith in the church a long time ago and shows Jesus dead as its triumph. Nobody re-alizes what enormous power this symbol represents. The System in its uniqueness and astonishing precision (well, it is a "super mind") overruled everything that stood in the way. Mass is spreading and creating bigger and bigger shadows. Shadow starts to spread itself all around.

Two other people were crucified together with Jesus, placed on the left and on the right of him. We can perceive them symbolically as representatives of the male and the female principles. One of them, on the right hand of Jesus, had denounced Jesus until his last breath. This is the male principle which separates and reigns. Not even in the face of death, did he recognize his behavior and was "blind" like the Mind. Therefore, he symbolically lost his right eye. The condemned man on the left hand of Jesus had reached awareness and represents the female principle, which is connecting and uniting. As soon as Jesus recognized his realization, he said to him:

"Truly, I say to you, today you will be with me in Paradise."
Luke 23,43

Because of events that are coming, faith in its essence will be reborn very soon. Exactly because of the need to create one's own reality. This will happen also thanks to archeological discoveries which will come and will be published, thanks to mysteries that have been hidden for two thousand years, knowledge which has been concealed or distorted.

A great inflow of awareness that has been going on roughly from the half of the past century is spreading inevitably. In the past two thousand years there have not been so many conscious people as there are today.

Why? The answer could be very extensive. Simply said, our space, our galaxy has reached the point of transformation where it has started to change. The male principle has reached its peak and now things have started to change.

It is not a coincidence that only in 1950 Pope Pius XII invoked the dogma of "the Assumption of Mary" which means that only from that year a full appreciation (dogma) of the female principle was irreversibly anchored in faith. Roughly in the 3rd century A.D., Christianity had started to unify itself by force. Until that time it had not been united and that happened at the councils called by the emperor Constantine the Great.

Until then, in some cases faith was different than what is presented by the church today. Many books and texts were destroyed but many were also hidden at various unexpected places of this planet. These old papers will soon be found and lead to the transformation of consciousness of the church itself and of all believers. **The house whose foundation was built on sand will be knocked down by water (information) and its fall will be great…**

The Marian dogmas – in this way the church inscribes its decisions about Mary – were dealt with in the 3rd and the 4th centuries A.D. It was in fact an interpretation of motherhood and virginity. It is not possible to either hide or manipulate motherhood, while virginity – connected with sex – is. It is not a secret that Mary was pregnant already before she was with Josef. If we consider other ways of conception than through the Holy Spirit, presented by church exclusively, then Jesus' father was probably another man than Josef. Then also Jesus' genealogy does not correspond with the Jewish tradition and with the "conditions" to be recognized as the Messiah.

These are ancient religious conflicts between Jews and Christians. Jews have not recognized Jesus as the Messiah.

It was not a problem in the Old Testament if a prophet was an "ordinary" person who somehow got into contact either with God himself or with his messengers (angels). It was necessary to distinguish, respectively to name (explain) the abilities that Jesus had and which are described in the Gospels. The only explanation acceptable for the minds of people of those times was his divinity in the sense that he is the son of God. With the meaning that he is the true son. (In this way, all baptized Christians are identified as if they are baptized by the Holy Spirit – they are God's children).

Let us go further, another Marian dogma from 1854 where it is said that "...the most Blessed Virgin Mary, from the first moment of her conception, by a singular grace and privilege from Almighty God and in view of the merits of Jesus Christ, was kept free of every stain of original sin." Through all this, the church has been gradually "purifying" feminity which has been appearing in some parts of their own Christian teachings (even until today).

The last dogma is, from our point of view, the most important because it has allowed the gate to the light and truth to be opened. It was the dogma about the "Assumption of Virgin Mary" from the year 1950.

Maybe you still see this as a coincidence or just a concurrence, but roughly from this time news about observations of UFO's started appearing. Humans also started to fly to outer space. As if something, a curtain or a lock was uncovered and new contact with the surroundings began.

Let us briefly look at the development of some attributes of current Christianity. Around 300 A.D. the sign of the cross started to be used as "crossing oneself" (locking of faith – see further) and around 500 A.D. priests started to dress themselves differently than other people (the mind prevailed – the male principle, the separating one). In the year 1079, priest's celibacy was established (the intangible processes of sex were understood and confirmed). The Inquisition started to aet around 1184 (it was necessary to "purify" the system). In 1870 The Pope's inerrability was officially acknowledged.

I have chosen only a few pieces of freely accessible information. As an interesting fact, the last one is that Mary was acknowledged to be the Mother of the Church in 1965.

Concerning the sign of the cross as it is taught in the catechism. The "small" cross: with the thumb of the right hand on the forehead, mouth and chest (during evangelium), the "big" cross: with the right hand from the forehead to the chest and from the left shoulder to the right one. The left hand is at the breast at the same time.

What are believers prompted to do in fact? More crosses at the same time represent a rail. Be aware here of the fact that the thumb, from the fingers' symbology point of view, belongs to the head, to the mind. Who stands behind this?

The cross at the forehead locks extra sensory perception, the cross at mouth communication and the cross at the chest locks the presence (infinity). These are the sixth, the fifth and the fourth gates (also the third and the second at the same time)...

You can find a certain symbology of the trinity of crosses within the body if you realize what centers of the human body enable divine power (to appear). It is the cross in the area of the fifth and the sixth gates (see the chapter Word). Then it is the cross in the area of the pelvis, the second gate. We have described their power already. Considering time and spatial context, we can liken the system of the energy gates (chakras) with the flow of time from the past (below) across the presence to the future. Similarly as the path from wanting (intangible world, ego-soul-the female aspect) across transformation (feelings) to thoughts, visions, to realization (the tangible world).

From the point of view of faith, as an aspect of the mind which serves the purpose of mastering the divine principles and creating your own reality, the above mentioned obscurities are not substantial. But the rituals themselves still carry the energy-information element inside.

Simply stated, current interpretations are so far from reality that is hard to say which one is more false. For us it is important to pick up the crux of the truth that have remained unchanged.

The message of the Holy Grail is without a doubt feminity, the female aspect, the female principle – applied or interpreted from various points of view. Let us finish this theme with the last quotation:

"Talitha cúmí!", which means: "Little girl, get up!"
Mark 5,41

The direct power of the word pronounced in the present by Jesus as an entirely conscious being.

The female principle is what will open the way to the inside. The mind, the male principle, and soul, the female principle, only in consent, in oneness have the ability to create.

It is no longer a mystery, that the teachings spoken by Jesus, were also passed on in India, Tibet, China and so forth, where it has remained in a different form than in the Christian ("Constantine") way which we know in the Western world.

Who brought the teachings there and who developed them further? Although the church has complete information, for some reason it has not proclaimed publicly Jesus' life (approximately 14 years before his crucifixion) until his appearance in Palestine. It is similar with later activities of one his brothers – Judas. Who is in fact the saint from the West described in many Eastern sacred papers?

Why is this information hidden? It could be possible to find out the true situation of Jesus' family (the relationship with his mother and father) but also with Mary Magdalene, with Judas, with Thomas and with Peter and John. Soon, other truths which have not been known will be illuminated. Consciousness is spreading without any restraint.

Help

As I have said before, I am using Christian symbols and also examples from the Bible for two reasons. Firstly, because you have all been influenced by this religion. It is not about going to church regularly, but a certain tradition is deeply rooted in your subconscious, directly into your DNA, whether you want it or not.

The second reason is that this religion has drawn so much energy from so many people that it is necessary to get this energy back, using the power of the stated quotations. The odd feelings which you may experience when reading some of the Bibles' quotations are connected with this.

The deep guilt that is buried inside most people is a source of such feelings. For you it is now important to forgive (to dissolve) these feelings of guilt. Call them as mistakes and leave them in the past. Guilt requests victims and in this way one of the oldest relations called HELP arises. This word is another one which you should remember and be careful when you use it. **Helping creates a relationship. It is the relationship of the victim and the guilty party.** This relationship is another foundation for the loss of self-confidence as a natural state. If someone helps you, you are then grateful to him. He is guilty of your gratitude and you are a victim of his help. The doing of good has never brought anything useful. Only plenty of victims and guilty persons. This relationship has a certain particularity, the roles of victims and guilty ones change very quickly. **They are not given "firmly".** Only the relationship itself is given firmly. Inside the relationship the roles change spontaneously. You are a victim for a moment and then guilty for a moment, according to whether you realize what is happening or not. This is not perceivable from the outside.

As you will gradually perceive the power of the word and be observing reality, you will start to understand the above stated information. It is about how you name your activity, if you use the word help then you will not reach what you wanted (if the purpose was the true attempt to teach someone and show him the way.)

Sensations, Feelings, Emotions

Here we will explain how humans are being influenced. You already know that manipulation comes through the third body gate (solar plexus). You also know that the mind in the human body is realized in three places. It is the place of the third gate where the mind is realized at its most intangible level. The second place is in the back part of head (the small, back brain) and the most tangible place in the front part of head (the big, front brain). This front brain is divided into two parts (hemispheres) – the right and the left. The left hemisphere controls the right half of the body and the right hemisphere controls the left part of the body. The aspects of female and male principle are mixed (crossed) here.

We said that in the area of the third gate the mind is placed at the most intangible level, the mind which is able to communicate with the soul that is also at the same place. Through harmony of both the mind and soul, faith arises. Through disharmony fear occurs. Fear has many aspects. It is in fact, also a belief but somehow distorted – from our point of view of the transformation of consciousness. We can perceive fear in this case as belief (in) that everything (something) will go "wrong".

This is the place through which present creatures can control the mind. It is necessary to add that both the mind and ego of an unconscious human being are "willing" to assist this manipulation. Why, if they are our allies? They, in fact, work "for us" all the time but we are not aware of it. More precisely said – we are not aware of the fact that what we do "inside" has a direct impact on what is happening outside – in our reality. This means that both mind and ego cooperate and work – for us – on "wrong" orders because they perceive such settings as our decisions.

It is the same as if you have a big company and don't pay enough attention to security rules. Your receptionist will let a criminal in. You, of course, perceive it as her mistake but if you look at the regulations you gave her, you then realize that she did not break any of them. Criminals have not introduced themselves as criminals, they behaved as if they knew the environment, as if they were "right at home" and they went to an elevator and were gone in a moment.

Let's describe the whole process using a simple schema. From the left comes an energy-information wave, we will call it a sensation. It comes into the body. This is the main moment. After it enters the body, it is transmuted into a feeling. How? It enters through the third gate and is modified by the first level of the mind. It is modified in a range from belief to fear, as we have described earlier. From here, this feeling travels to the next part of the mind – the small brain where the movie, mentioned in the first part of this book, is projected. Sensation influenced or maybe manipulated by vibration of the third body gate is screened. Sensation is screened already as a feeling. Who "is watching" this movie? It is another part of the mind (big brain). It is "the mind" we have in fact been talking about until now. The body reacts by emotions (in some cases) to this mind.

Focus well now. I have stated that sensation (an energy-information wave from the outside) comes into the body and transforms itself into a feeling (frequency influenced by the mind). Now the ego comes onto the scene, the ego which is "a communication tool" between the own being (soul) and the mind (physical body). If the soul is in harmony, in oneness, in balance with mind, then this sensation is transmuted (by mind in the third gate) to the feeling which is transmuted (by mind in the small brain) into a movie and the movie is dubbed by ego. **Ego will add the words!** Now you have the complete picture. Which words ego adds depends on the kind of energy that comes to the small brain, energy of faith or fear. This "sounded" movie, or rather a movie with a commentary (explanation) of ego, is then transformed (by the mind in the big brain which is "a spectator" of that movie) to final energy. What this energy will be like depends, above all, on "an agreement" between ego and mind. If a feeling goes through the body and is not stopped by any disharmony, disunity or imbalance, then it leaves through the back body gate in the form of free will. Which is pure energy of oneness of mind and soul, the kind of energy which creates ("secretly", intangibly) your reality. But if this energy is "trapped" in body, emotion is the result.

I have described very complex processes very simply, where the result is in fact influenced by more factors. In principle (and this is what is now important for us), it is possible to describe this intangible process in this way. As I said in the Introduction, we do not need exact definitions of particular processes, we just need to understand them and use them for our own creation of reality.

To clarify and make the process transparent, I will repeat once again how intangible vibrations are transformed into tangible ones via human beings. The way you create reality. You know that the human mind is an intangible entity. The human body is tangible and the mind is intangible. The mind is realized (created) in the human body in three parts. Out of these three parts, the least tangible (the most intangible) part is placed in the area of the third gate (solar plexus). Through this area, a frequency from the outside is taken in and transformed (either by faith or fear) so that it can go to the second part of the mind, to the small brain where it is transformed with the assistance of ego to another kind of energy which is more tangible. From here, a frequency – which is now tangible ("action of a movie" commented by ego) travels to the third part of the mind, to the big brain which, after watching a movie, will then send signals to the physical body. Out of these signals, either emotion or free will is created.

Emotion, as we clarified earlier, is poison for the physical body. It is a frequency arising from disharmony between the mind and soul. But if harmony occurs, then energy is transformed into free will. And this is what we are interested in.

Energy of Free Will

How to create free will and what is it? First of all, as you already know, it is necessary not to create emotions. Not to allow present creatures to manipulate you. If you do not do so, then you are getting the mind and soul into harmony, as described above.

The best is to practice all the explained principles in your everyday life. This way you will gain assurance, faith that it works. You will overcome obstacles, walk through the narrow gate and you will be able to create.

Start with applying everything from the first part of the book. In the moment when you start observing coming emotions and you don't allow them to influence you; certain stillness will arise inside you. This stillness will enable the body to function according to its own intelligence. This is important because the body and its intangible representative – the mind, are the ones with whom you will be seeking and finding balance. As soon as you start you will be receiving "signs". Signs are a kind of "coincidence" which will start to play out in your surroundings. The stronger your faith and the weaker your fear is, the more you will be in balance and witness the more obvious signs. How will you recognize such signs? You will definitely recognize them when they come. For others, these will be only common things and only you will see something unearthly in them. For example in a moment when you will be dealing with some thought concerning the transformation of consciousness, something that will draw your attention will happen. Perhaps a dog will bark, a car will blow its horn or glass will break somewhere. You will be walking along the street and dealing with some theme which is connected with it. Suddenly you will hear a fragment of someone's conversation which will give you the answer. You will meet people who will smile at you in the moment which will be special for you considering what you were dealing with at the moment. You will see writing on a wall, an advertising slogan which will suddenly match your crossword. This will be only the beginning. You will meet new people. Why? You will start to radiate different vibrations than before. Some people will disappear from your life, as darkness disappears in the presence of light. You will feel a great inflow of energy if you end your enslavement to present creatures. You will start to notice people differently than before. You will be looking at them as if you are seeing them for the first time. They will look differently; maybe they will even behave differently. It will not be because of them, it will happen because of you. You will see and perceive them much more widely than before. You will see what you have not seen before, although it was there already. Still believe in yourself, your instincts. Maybe you will start hearing birds singing in the park, birds which may have not been there before. You will notice flowers. All this and much more will be accompanying your process of realizing. Signs will be more fierce and with a deeper influence. **Do not resist, do not let the mind resist = to be afraid. Become observers of all what is around you. Be passers-by; do not attach yourself to anything**. You will see that you do not need to be in a hurry and stressed. Open your eyes and breathe in. Look outside around you. Your reality may be transforming already in these moments. You can see it through your eyes, colors are different, you cannot describe it, but something has changed. It may even scare you at first, but do not worry about it, be still. Only sense in the stillness of presence. Let the world communicate with you, to show you what you have not seen until now. Relax and sense yourself as a part of an entire being. You are in absolute stillness and harmony with everything. Observe flowers, trees how still they are, but full of life.

Try to be aware of what you need. Not of what you want but what you really need. Wanting is a matter of ego which feels it is the one who makes decisions. Need is the real will of the own being (soul) that is a signpost of life's journey. You may be surprised how little you need in fact. It is because your soul is not used to speaking about its needs freely. Give time to this process. Discover yourself step by step, do not hurry, and do not suffer from pressure. It would again be the mind and its fear that "it" does not work.

According to what phase of consciousness you are in, how present you are, determines how "fast" you can be in creating reality around you. In the beginning, there is a longer time from the order to the realization. This is the stumbling block of many people, who simply under the pressure of the mind don't last. That is why it is important to free yourself from influences of present creatures that always work with the frequency of fear, before you start to create. So, if you are trying to create your reality, then be patient. In the beginning be happy with perceiving signs, which are in fact angels, messengers of your changing reality. If you do not perceive signs, then ease up your attention. It is not about attention, because it is not possible to overlook the signs. It is more about that you are not given any signs (better said, you are not yet able to recognize them), which means that you are not free at all – you are controlled by mind and fear. If this has disturbed you, then you can be sure that it is true. Go back to the beginning and find more humility and sincerity. If you sometimes think that you can perceive something, then you are on the right path. The key is not to press, not to hurry, not to want everything in a moment. Just be and try to create only as if it was by the way. Set your goals and intentions, imagine that it has happened already and enjoy dreaming.

If something goes right, enjoy it; be aware that it is proof of your creation of reality. If something does not go right, enjoy it too (see the shirt and the coat). Enjoy non-success because you know that is a success in reality. You have set something negative sometime in the past and it has come now. Hurray, because if you do not react negatively to such an event, it will interrupt this negation (karma) and the next time such a moment will be of a joyful frequency which you are just experiencing. Negation will not be repeated because you have stopped and dissolved the curse this time, by accepting, forgiving, loving and joy. As if you were purifying negative thoughts (both conscious and unconscious) from the past. Dissolve them by light, joy and darkness (sorrow, negation) will disappear. If you do not request it, it will not come back. This purification can take quite a long time but has its end and its frequency will diminish and then disappear entirely. This training is not purposeless. If you work with fantasy, with imagination, with dreaming (with open eyes), then these frequencies are created by the mind. The part of the mind which we have spoken about as of the big brain. If the brain is creating these images, then it "does not have time" to create emotions. This is the little "trick" that will make your start of creating easier. Just be careful not to have too intense images (which is very easy) because they could be projected reversely to your body and their non fulfillment could later bring frustration and disappointment. Just play a little bit, it is not a suggestion neither power of thought that will create.

It is free will by which you create. The kind of energy which is either transformed to emotion or leaves the body as free will and influences reality. This way information about what is below (inside) will get to what is above (outside). This is the way of creation. So "easy" it is.

Just try it out, play. Who plays, doesn't get into trouble, this pays for the mind too. The more often you consciously imagine how you will be creating, the less often the mind will have the chance to create fears and trap energy in the body. Another little weight on an imaginary scale of mind and soul. Considering how everything is connected, you will prosper from each such step in two ways.

Frequency (sensation) comes into the body, goes through particular levels of the mind (feeling) and leaves the body in the form of free will. You see that this graphic picture represents an early Christian symbol (a fish).

Frequency is trapped in the body and feeling is transformed into emotion (free will is blocked).

Firstly, that you do not have to deal with the fears of the mind and secondly in the way that the mind casually gets to a better balance, which again diminishes the possibility to be controlled. Like this it will repeat more intensely, like a spiral. Unify the male and female principles; it is the symbol of a spiral.

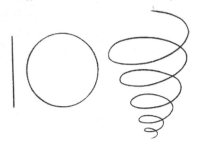

The potential of the male principle is symbolized by a line, unifying the influence of the female principle symbolized by a circle. Through the connection of these two principles a spiral is born, as the symbol of creation. In different variations you can see this symbol all around you, from DNA to galaxies in space.

As I have said, many people are discouraged that "nothing is happening". Hold on and be firm in your faith. Each of your orders will come into existence, it only depends how long it will take. These are the coming "good" and "bad" news which are sometimes hard to understand. Each of them is connected, has its cause (curse of causality) in a certain state of your consciousness when you created (unconsciously, out of presence). Because this state of consciousness varies, also the own realization is somehow (from the time point of view) nonsense. In presence, you are more conscious or less conscious. In other words, sometimes you are more present. It means that something will happen sooner and something later but which does not correspond with the chronological moment of the order. Such disunity often brings doubts.

How to overcome them? Besides that you will be entirely conscious all the time? There is also a certain "twist" to it. Take everything that happens to you as good news. Make it a game. Enjoy all bad news contrary to any coincidences. Have fun from all the uncomprehending looks of those who do not know what you are doing. Laugh anytime you do not accomplish something. Do not make a tragedy of it. Everything has its own sense which you do not have to understand immediately. It is enough if you accept it as a fact. Not to judge and not to label it, not to create any conclusions. Was something supposed to have gone wrong? It would not have gone well even if you had stood on your head (mind). If it is supposed to go well, it will go well because it is your course. The closer you get to yourself, the closer you will be on your course, on your mission – which is "supposed to go well". The closer you are, the fewer obstacles there will be. You will walk forward along your path without any problems. That something is still not going well? Then you are either doing it "incorrectly" or you are there "wrongly" (at the wrong place). It is not exactly like that because wrong or well are terms and interpretations of the mind. You were supposed to realize something and you would not have come to it without such experience. Everything happens "well".

"Do not judge, and you will not be judged. Do not condemn, and you will not be condemned. Forgive, and you will be forgiven. Give, and it will be given to you. A good measure, pressed down, shaken together and running over, will be poured into your lap. For with the measure you use, it will be measured to you."
Luk 6,37

Simply enjoy yourself, allow it and you will find out that you can be happier now, not sometime in the future; when you have a better job, more money, a paid mortgage, grown children and so on. It is in fact not possible to be happy at any other time than right now. Leave the hell of the mind and make the mind your ally; put it back to its right position.

It is not possible to have an ally that would fill you with fear anytime you are making a decision. You live in dissatisfaction and expectation, you are not content, something is still missing. What is it? Is it faith? No. It is fear. You need faith. Not in a religious context but faith in yourself, that you can be satisfied. You will not find satisfaction through earthly possessions. A new car will satisfy you only for a moment, as will a new lover. Everything is satisfactory only for a short time to feed your senses and also mind for a moment, but the mind will speak again after a while. You are full of doubts and fear. So, you will find another goal that will certainly satisfy you; a new luxurious watch, a new higher position at work, a sport which you will really enjoy. Nothing at all, the path does not lead this way. Be aware that the mind causes this lack of fulfillment.

"No good tree bears bad fruit, nor does a bad tree bear good fruit. Each tree is recognized by its own fruit."
Luk 6,43

If your mind does not allow you to be happy, then it cannot be that "good" which will protect you and lead you through life. What do you say? Just try it and go back to the first part of this book – practice and observe.

In the moment you allow yourself to sense, signs will come and they will give you an urge to try this further. Do not forget about the power of the word, whether for your benefit or vice versa. Do not be angry if something goes wrong. You may not succeed immediately but keep trying. Getting angry is also emotion, a body reaction to the unsatisfied mind which did not get what it had assumed it would get.

Free yourself. Be present all the time and the number of places that you create consciously (good) will be increasing gradually. Then the realizations will also be "good" more and more often. There will be less places where you will be creating unconsciously (wrongly) and of course less realizations of such unconscious creations. This means that your life situation will get generally better. There will also be dark places not illuminated by presence but you will overcome such places with a smile and this way you will dissolve them like light dissolves darkness. Because if you do not react negatively to them, no negation will be set for future creation, and they will then disappear effortlessly. You will not be negative inside and therefore you will not set any negative realization on the outside.

This is the principle and the mystery of the cross. This is the application of divine principles in practice. Just keep trying it – on and on. Results will come and if you are not too eager to see them, then they will come surprisingly soon and in a great amount.

How is it possible that something can happen "just like that"? How to explain all the signs, coincidences that you have experienced?

For that – the mind (which asks) can grasp a simple explanation of existence itself.

Existence, all what was, is and will be, is infinite. There are all variants contained which we can imagine; absolutely all of them, because infinitely many is really a lot. In existence, there are also all variants of other people. If you decide that something will be different, then your presence will move to the place of existence which corresponds to your image. You will become travelers of space that is a more exact description rather than travelers of time.

Everything that happens, everything that exists, moves around certain places in existence. The presumption that you stand at one place and everything moves around you is similar to the hypothesis that the Sun moves around the Earth. Time does not exist in existence. If your mind grasps this then it will stop being disturbed by terms like infinity or by questions like: "What was before and what is around, beyond space?" You will understand the sense of the question "Where?" compared to the question "When?" did it happen.

Time is not in existence, there is only presence. Our reality is a part of existence, something like a subset. All options of action already exist and have always existed. Our reality only moves around particular places of existence. Its movement is determined by consciousness of beings that exist in it.

I will describe this with the following example. This reality is like a big plane. People are like passengers of this plane who can influence the plane's direction and speed. Only the conscious ones can, the rest sit in the back and think that in the front it is the same as in the back, that nothing can be influenced there. The ones who sit on the left side argue with those who sit on the right side about what they see from the window (like fleas in our example).

The first ones do not believe the others and all of them are in fact right. In the front are the conscious ones. Consciousness is like an ability to program the autopilot which operates the plane. The more there are conscious ones, the longer the stage of the journey is possible to program. The Mayan calendar was created like this. These human beings were the last ones of sufficient numbers of the conscious to create reality (the future) and they had set it to the end of their calendar. The so much discussed date of the year 2012 actually comes from this – from the end of the Mayan calendar. The autopilot program is coming to an end. Since then, there have not been enough conscious human beings to create the reality further.

Existence is complete, perfect. Some can call it God. There are all possibilities, all variants contained in it. If you decide and create your reality, then the whole reality will move to the place of existence where for others the situation remains the same but for you it is the way you wanted it. The problem is not if everyone will be creating like this, the possibilities are infinite. Everything is happening in the present, only in the present. Time does not exist. Yes, successive time exists, you can count particular stages, create hours and a calendar. Beware of the misleading sense of such comparisons.

So, if you know how a macrocosm, existence looks like, then it is more understandable for the mind, that it is possible to influence it, that it is natural. Oneness of mind and soul is the key.

Try to realize your needs and you will see that it can be done. How should you realize them? It is easy or it can be easy if you allow it yourself. Simply do not doubt that it will happen. Believe that what you need will simply come to be. What is preventing you from believing it? The mind. The mind hesitates, doubts and is afraid all the time. But you are not the mind. It is only a part of your body. You need it on your side, not for telling you what is and is not possible, not for fighting with it. This is the work which nobody else can do for you. You yourself can take your freedom back. You will be rewarded with everything that I have described. How long will it take? It depends only on you. I know people who were able to do it in several months, but also others who have been trying already for several years.

What role does your ego play in all this? Absolutely crucial. Ego is in fact the one who "secretly" encourages the mind to boycott your efforts. This happens in the small brain. Ego as the present entity wants to be, and wants to be the highest one. It is much more sophistica-ted than the mind. Mind is "the good old guy" of the type one plus one equals two. Ego is the player who stands in the back and pulls the strings.

Ego is a part of the own being which is separated. That is why you communicate with yourself with such dif-ficulty – the mind with the soul. Ego has emancipated itself and feels independent. It is supported by many other "external" present creatures. It was really a foolish thing to do to separate, led by the male principle (which was a tool of ancient gods shepherd.) This division trou-bles and tortures ego the most. Ego is not complete; it is separated and feels to be incomplete. Its nature is to be like an engine, drafter, a gate for the spirit, for movement and creation. But what is an engine without a car? It only whirrs without any satisfaction. It has found an ally – the mind that controls the body. The ego via the mind pushes the body to completely inconvenient situations and the mind, which can "figure it out", is afraid; its fear is the same as ego's. That fear which is injected, inserted into the body through the third gate.

Do you understand this chaos already? These entities are stuck in themselves and now they kick around and do not know what to do. Like many people are. Out of their inner "emotions" something like super-creatures were created which then started to control them. They have arisen out of this free energy (see the chapter on Gods shepherds).

Save them and you save yourselves. Observe them at first, then start to communicate and later on they will again become a part of you.

Save ego by not identifying yourselves with its opinions and judgments. You will not jump into traps set by present creatures. **Surrender your own importance** which is the most difficult thing to do because the existence of mutated (controlled) ego dwells in it – in your importance. Show another face. Surrender and forgive. Nobody else can do this for you, **only the son of man has the power to stop this curse,** this sin.

A source of misunderstanding and of negative power is hidden somewhere there. It is again the female principle which leads us through like the more and more present message of the Holy Grail. In the Old Testament, god says to the snake:

"And I will put enmity between you and the woman, and between your offspring and hers; she will crush your head."
Genesis 3,15 (1st Book of Moses)

The main power is fear that comes via the mind. Liberate your mind through information and inspiration which the female principle brings. Let it "crush your head", to stop the mind from creating fear and emotions and bring the mind back to perfection, to perfection represented by human beings.

Everything is connected with everything and the deeper you will grasp the principles of functioning in this reality, the more you will perceive how everything is connected. My descriptions are, although I have tried hard, still strictly separate. I have described particular processes separately for a better understanding of the processes themselves. I have connected them later on and like that we are getting closer to the real state. However, preceding examples do not have to then correspond with your actual state of consciousness, which is at a higher level already. I have been making these slight inaccuracies and using simple and purposeful examples in order to pass on basic information as quickly as possible.

This book has described the basis of the transformation of consciousness but it contains the truths that have the highest power. Our reality is heading towards a certain point in existence in which it will change. The more conscious human beings are at the time, the greater participation we will have in the creation of the new coming reality.

Epilogue of the Second Part

Roughly during the 1950's of the last century, a substantial shift in human consciousness took place. After the last manifestation of the male principle (world wars, concentration camps, atomic bombs and others), the female principle started coming back to this reality like rays of light. It came from the inside and together with it, courageous women started to appear more and more. Science and technology experienced a great boom. This happened thanks to the newly coming (reviving) female principle and its aspect – inspiration.

In these years, this reality was entered by people (they started to be born) who later in the seventies and eighties brought to this world a generation of so called indigo children – beings enlightened, who are creating a bridge (comeback) to the truth, they are creating heaven on earth.

These children are now in the third part (around the age of 21) of their development and are starting to create (giving birth) to entirely new human beings.

These new people are creating a new earth. They are descendents of people with the abilities that humans have always attributed only to gods.

The Son of man is coming!

The time is now.

Part Three

The Mystery of Creation – the Jewish Candlestick

In this last part, I am including a theoretical bonus. As we have already said, human beings naturally manage divine principles. So, it should also contain the "genetics" of the world's creation (of this reality).

It really is like that. We will expand our consciousness with other information. The symbol that will enable us to get in touch with the truth is the Jewish seven-branched candlestick. For Jews themselves, it is a greater symbol than David's shield (better known as the Star of David). It is interesting that the symbol of the David's shield is sometimes symbolized as the symbol of the fourth chakra (in Eastern spiritual systems). The deeper and closer we go, the more connections you will see between particular directions on this planet.

The seven-branched Jewish candlestick...

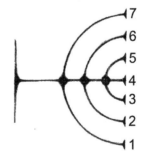

... is the symbol of the basic interconnection of the human body's energy gates.

For a full understanding of the further described connections it is necessary to find and perceive them in presence. The less the mind will trouble you with its logic, the more you will find out...

We will again use extra sensory perception that will now work in parallel with sensory perception – reading. We will also use the power of the cross in both positions, as we have described them before.

Let us turn the candlestick (used now only as a graphic symbol), the way it is shown on the picture.

We can see that if we connect the symbol to the picture of a human body, the particular branches show us how the energy centers of human body are connected in an

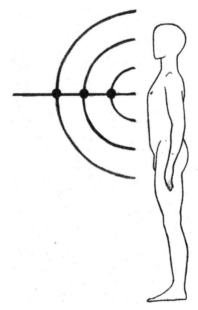

A candlestick as a symbol of essential interconnections of energy gates of the human body.

essential way. We will now call them gates. We can see that the first gate is connected with the seventh gate. The same as the second gate is connected with the sixth, and the third gate is connected with the fifth. The only independent one, in this sense, is the fourth gate.

For better clarity we will now work only with symbols. On the next picture you can see how the Holy Trinity is mapped into the points where connections of the gate cross with the track of the fourth gate. We will call these cross points seals. Why I call them the Holy Trinity you will understand from the picture where we will give spi-

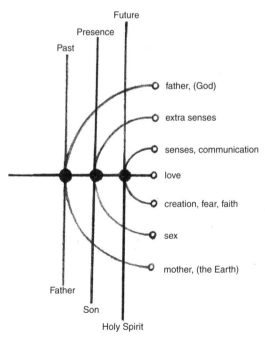

A description of the energy gates and their cross points for the transformation of consciousness purposes.

ritual dimension to the particular seals. At the first seal there is the Holy Father, the Son at the second and the Holy Spirit at the third. What it means in clear speech is stated above. It is the past, the present and the future. It is clear that the left is the past and the right is the future. Our movement in time along the cross is from the left to the right. Now we will stop and look at the single gates and the seals related to them.

To be able to open the fourth gate and go "further" it is necessary to put three seals together. For compilation of each seal you need to get both of its halves which are hidden behind the corresponding body gates.

It is clear that to put the first seal together, the key to the first gate needs to be acquired, which represents the relationship with your mother.

I want to point out here two well-known state-ments. The first one is: "**Honor your mother and your father**." The second one begins: "Our Father who art in heaven…" Notice that the first statement mentions your mother and your father, so it pronounces (creates) for each of them individually, independently. It respects in-dividuality, a person. Which is a free approach. On the other hand, the second statement says "**our Father**" and withdraws freedom from individuality, transforms humans (people) to the flock which repeats (does not create) the same over and over. Because relationships are always between one element and a second element. As we have described in the chapter about children, it is not possible to keep more elements (components) in one position. The result is that the repetition of this phrase (statement) strengthens manipulative (enslaving) power over people who voluntarily pronounce "our Father" while a free version of this statement would be: "**my Father**". It is necessary to harmonize the relationship with your mother. To understand and accept what she has done, become god and forgive her, because she then will forgive you. In the moment when you do this, you will get one half of the seal. You need to do the same in the relationship with your father. You will get the second half of the seal. In this moment we have the first seal of the Trinity relating to the past open. We can deal with any situation from the past of this embodiment and of previous embodiments (karma connections, causality). Finish all the curses from the past.

The second gate is connected with sex and on the picture you can see its interconnection with the sixth gate, which is the center of extra sensory perception. It is obvious that these two seemingly different areas are in fact directly connected (I am indicating them like that on purpose). You have learned more in the chapter about sex. If you reach harmony of these two gates, you will put two halves of the seal in their place and the present will be open for you, presence with its entire power. As you can see on the picture, it is the second seal of the Holy Trinity, presence, position of the "Son". Through harmony, balance of particular gates you will achieve having the seal in the right place. You will use here the principle of the triangle in the same way as we have explained in the chapter about children. It is necessary to work evenly with chakras otherwise the gates will not open. Any disharmony (higher or lower function) of one gate will cause a distortion of the triangle's peak away from the position of the Holy Trinity seal.

271

To walk through the fourth gate (the gate of four elements, of love and eternity) it is necessary to obtain the last (third) seal. The third gate is guarded by the mind and fear. It is directly connected with the ability to communicate, with the fifth gate which also contains the five tangible senses. If you succeed to get keys to those gates, you will obtain the last seal which opens the gate to the future, to the (not yet) realized part of existence. With this you have walked to the fourth gate. Through this gate it is possible to walk to another part of reality, to its other dimension, intangibl.

You surely understand that what I have described above would fill a single book. Such a journey begins with many hours of work the best is to practice with someone who is at a substantially higher level of consciousness.

It is not the intention of this book to describe this activity in detail because such an activity is at another level of the transformation of consciousness for which it is good to manage the initial skill. The initial skill is the ability to maintain freedom in relation towards at least some present creatures.

At the end of this book we will talk a bit more about the creation of this reality, principles and symbols itself. As I said previously, human beings contain information about their own creation. Now free yourself from wanting to know and understand everything immediately.

On the next picture you can see that if we draw in the same way a connection between tangible reality into intangible reality, we will gain an integrated picture of a circle.

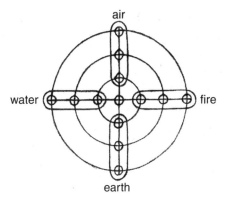

air

water — fire

earth

If we project the tangible (that which is on the left) to the intangible (that which is on the right), we will again get the symbol of the cross. If we unify the particular parts (gates) into trinities – we will get the symbol of creation of this reality by the four elements.

We have been using the principle that which is above is that which is below and this is one of the principles of the cross. It is visible at the seven gates of the body. In the same way we apply that which is on the left to that which is on the right.

Let us not deal now with concrete things. I understand that it is not yet easy for you, but let us focus on principles. We are going to the very beginning of being. The picture indicates a connection between particular gates and elements. You see how particular gates get together in trinities and elements are created. If we connect particular points by lines, then similarity with a pyramid is obvious.

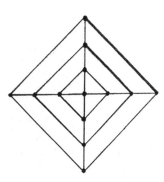

If we connect particular points (elements), the symbol of a pyramid arises.

Now, let us turn the cross to the left to the position of "X". You will get division (connection) to two basic principles, the male and the female. If you turn the cross to the right to the position of "X", you will get two pillars that support existence, two trees in Paradise or two pillars of the Solomon temple.

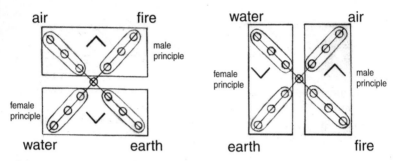

Through the connection of two elements belonging to the respective principle we will simplify relations in this reality to two basic principles (male and female).

The last simplification leads to the number one. Unity of chaos, Tao, God, Existence...

Look at the other pictures and see how the symbols are connected, how they complement each other and where everywhere the truth of creation is hidden ...

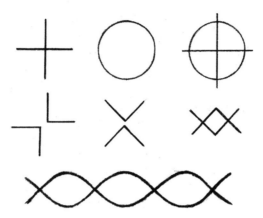

A circle as the symbol of unity is divided by the cross (space/time) into four elements. At the same time, it contains the inner (female) and the outer (male). If we divide the cross we will get the symbols for the male and the female principles. If we reconnect (movement...) these symbols, a helix (spiral) appears.

Spirals are more or less hidden in many religious symbols.

Each energy centre (chakra = a circle) has a male and a female aspect. If you give them circle shapes you can see very interesting connections and graphical symbols. One example for all: the element of water (the female principle) represents a drop. Its shape is the same as the shape of the flame (the male principle) which represents the element of fire. On the picture you can see that they have the opposite orientation (not only inside the circle of the fourth gate).

If you connect the drop and the flame (the female and the male principle) the symbol of infinity or the symbol of the heart arises...

So much is the theoretical bonus. For some of you it may be an inspiration to go further and read other books or potentially start to realize and create. Do not forget **freedom = unconditionality**. Freedom in your personal world, in your reality, can only exist if it is not contingent on anyone or anything.

Jesus said: "Who acknowledged everything but has a lack in himself, will have lack in everything."

In conclusion, there is only left to say that many books full of theories have already been written. Not only knowledge, but above all skills, will take you to higher levels of consciousness where you can encounter new facts and unexpected connections...

NOTES:

NOTES:

NOTES:

NOTES:

NOTES:

NOTES:

NOTES:

NOTES:

NOTES:

If you want to contact
Publishing Keltner
for more information:

publishing@keltner.cz

www.keltner.cz

Tomáš Keltner
The Transformation of Consciousness
The Mystery of the Cross

Cover & Drawings Marie Keltner
Translation Mgr. Monika Tomíčková
Graphic Layout and Typography Vladimír Vyskočil
Printed and Bound by PBtisk Příbram
Publishing Keltner

www.keltner.cz

ISBN 978-80-904708-2-8